Land of My Mothers

Carol Ann Lewis

ISBN:1518695396
ISBN-13:9781518695391

ALSO BY CAROL ANN LEWIS

CWMBRAN – HISTORY AND MYSTERY
GWENT HISTORY AND MYSTERY
VICTORIAN CWMBRAN
VICTORIAN PONTYPOOL
VICTORIAN DOMESTIC ABUSE
TELL THEM OF US
HAUNTING TALES
CHILDREN OF NATURE – A HISTORY OF WITCHES
CHRISTMAS PAST
CHRISTMAS IN MONMOUTHSHIRE
DREAMS – THE FORGOTTEN CRAFT
HANBURY PARK
EDINA GREEN IN THE AFTERLIFE

ALL AVAILABLE FROM AMAZON OR AS A DOWNLOAD TO KINDLE

FOLLOW ME ON TWITTER @CAROLANNLEWIS1

i

INTRODUCTION

During my studies with the University of South Wales, I have become fascinated with the history of Wales and an area I have become particularly interested in, is women's history. You know? That history of the other half of the human race that so often gets sidelined. Womens history I have found is the most difficult to write about, mostly due to a lack of information. If we compare the history of the human race to two ships, one for men and one for women, sailing on an ocean of time, the men's ship has survived and reached us with all its history mostly intact. The women's ship however has been prone to attacks, her stories lost or simply not recorded and as historians we can only stand in the harbour and rescue as many snippets as we can from her, shout into the void and hope someone answers.

While researching this book and collecting articles from Victorian newspapers, it has struck me that women of that time were tough, resilient and feisty. They were hard working, creative and talented. They also had to face the most terrible hardships, often alone, for which they would then also be blamed. I hope you will enjoy the following accounts of women's lives in Wales. I hope it may also inspire you to find out more about other forgotten women.

CHILDHOOD

Ann Lewis

One October morning in 1838, Ann, aged 5, the daughter of Thomas Lewis, a widower of Talywain, while in the act of taking a kettle off the fire caught her clothes in the flames. Neighbours rushed to help her, no doubt hearing her cries but she was so badly burned before they could extinguish the flames that she died the same night.

Baby Morgan

Childhood, not an experience given to all. In December 1842 a female infant was found dead in a field near the canal in Pontypool. An inquest was held on the body and the verdict was that the child was born alive and death occurred by injuries to her head. Suspicion immediately fell upon the mother, Sarah Morgan. She was apprehended, partially examined and admitted the child was hers but it had been stillborn.

Mercy Biggs

In March 1856, Mercy, aged around 4 or 5, was playing with some other children in limekilns in Blaenavon when, it was supposed, she went to a part of the burning kiln to warm herself. Here her clothes caught fire. The other children raised the alarm and the father arrived at the spot and succeeded in extinguishing the flames by wrapping his coat around her. He took her home and sent for medical assistance but she was so burnt that upon trying to take her coat off her flesh came away too. She lingered for a few hours and died the same evening.

Mary Creel

Mary lived in Cwmbran, the daughter of a miner. The Illustrated Usk Observer, who recorded her story, described her as a 'little girl', so her age is uncertain. One January day in 1857, while her mother was absent, she went off into another house to play with some children. Here somehow her clothes caught fire and she was severely burnt. A young man by the name of 'Joy', on hearing her cries, went to put out the flames and in doing so burnt his hands so much so he was unable to work again. Mary, afterwards lay in a dangerous condition.

Mary Ann Burke

Mary Ann was the daughter of a coker. She drowned in the canal in Cwmbran in 1857, though it is not known how she got in there. She was only spotted because her cloak was found floating on top of the water. An inquest was held at Pontypool Town Hall before coroner William Brewer. Witness, Thomas Reid, lock keeper of Llanfrechfa said -

"I was at my work on the Monmouthshire Canal on Friday 24th April. A lad came to me and asked me to bring a hook as a little girl had fallen into a lock. I ran down and let the water out and with the hook I found the deceased in the bottom of the lock but she was quite dead. The boy told me that he had found a cape on top of the water."

Michael Burke, father, said -

"I am a fireman and box filler at the Cwmbran furnaces. On Friday, about one o clock, my wife sent deceased to the shop. She had to cross the lock over a piece of wood. My wife gave her five pence. One halfpenny was found on her when taken out of the canal. She had been away twenty minutes. I do not believe her death occurred from accident. She was eight years of age."

Verdict – Found dead in the canal.

Lot

In Blaenavon in November 1862 some gossip began to circulate around town that a young woman named Lot, who lived near the railway station had attempted to kill her baby. She had only just been delivered of the baby but it was said she had tried to bury it in soil in a water closet behind the house. One of her neighbours had heard the wailing of the baby and succeeded in rescuing it and therefore disclosed the affair. It was true the incident did occur but the baby fell in the closet accidentally. The seat was instantly removed by the girl's mother who quickly recovered the child and placed it in bed with the mother. The police were called but on hearing all the facts considered there to be no grounds for a charge.

Eliza Bryant

In Abersychan, in November 1862, Eliza's father and step mother were charged with ill treating and assaulting Eliza. Witness Eliza Rapps said -

"I live next door to the prisoners and I have frequently heard them ill-treating the child. I remonstrated with the female prisoner for doing so, when she told me to go into my house. I have seen the child black and blue from having been beaten. I saw her beaten a fortnight 'a gone', and have seen her put out of doors in the rain. I have seen the woman beat the oldest girl shamefully, and when her father came home at night he beat her with a rope. I told the mother that if the neighbours would help me I would put her into the river. The children were starved to death. One of them came to me crying and said that the mother wanted her to go and steal coal."

On the defendants being asked if they had any questions to ask the witness the female said, since I have been a wife to Joseph Bryant I have never raised my hand to Joseph Bryant's child and Joseph Bryant did not leave his children to me. Having proceeded in this strain for some time the chairman told the defendant she had made a long speech, she had to ask questions.

Another witness, Ann Paul, stated she had seen the child beaten by the female defendant, very severely with a stick about two months previously when she said -

"Martha, what are you going to do with the child?"

Witness had also seen the child beaten by the father and turned out of doors.

Witness Martha Greaves said she had seen the child picking crumbs out of the pig dung and had also seen her beaten by her step mother.

Mr Wainwright, relieving officer spoke of the emaciated condition of the child as exhibited before the Board of Guardians.

Mary Underwood said that she had never seen children treated in such a bad way in her life. She had heard them screaming for the past two months. On one occasion her lodger was attracted to the house by the cries of the eldest girl and on going in he saw the father beating her with the strap from his waist.

P.C Brown said -

"On Wednesday last, Mr Tucker, surgeon, called on me and said that there was a child in Valentine Row that was suffering from an insufficiency of food and ill-treatment. I went to the place and saw the child and never observed such an object in my life before. A woman brought it a basin of broth and it ate it quite ravenously and asked for more. The father of the child earns 12 to 13 shillings a week out of which he gets a 10s weekly draw; his son earns 12s and other money is made in the house by selling sand."

It was also stated that the female defendant pampered a child that she had had in her widowhood whilst she starved and neglected those to whom she was step mother. After a long incoherent statement from the step mother, that had very little to do with the case, the chairman told the defendant that the Bench thought they had been guilty of grossly ill-treating the child for which the step mother would be committed for six months and the man for four months in the House of Correction.

Mary Davies

Mary was the daughter of Edward Davies of Pengam near Blackwood. She was thirteen when she disappeared in October 1864.

She had been living with her grandmother, Mary Davies, in Tredunnock and had been sent on 22nd September to a well situated on the Newbridge side of the River Usk. She was not seen or heard from again. A search was made in the well and in the river but no trace of Mary or the tub she had taken with her was found, until, a few days later when the tub was found in the river near Caerleon. It was supposed Mary dropped the tub, it rolled down the hill from the well to the riverbank and on trying to retrieve it, she fell in the river and drowned. To account for the absence of a body it was thought it must have got stuck somewhere in the river and so a description was issued.

Mary was tall for her age, thin, light complexion and light brown hair. She was dressed in a brown frock with a black piece around the bottom, cotton summer bonnet and lace up boots.

Miss Lewis

A row erupted in Tredegar in June 1866 between Miss Lewis, who was described by the Monmouthshire Merlin as a 'young girl' and Mrs Marsden, a married woman. Lewis was said to have 'fired away in English'. At the court hearing though she was not able to speak English and so the whole trial was conducted in Welsh. She told the court she was walking down the street when Mrs Marsden rushed out of her house and struck her. Mrs Marsden, who was of 'good character' complained it was impossible to live near her and that she created disturbances with neighbours. The case was dismissed.

Mary Thomas

Mary was the daughter of Thomas Thomas and step daughter of Sarah Thomas. She lived in Usk and in February 1868, when she was aged eleven, her parents were brought before the court on charges of cruelty. The court heard that Mary often went without food. Sometimes her father gave her only bread and water. Her step mother whipped her and rubbed salt into her wounds. She also beat her with a cane to which the father was reported to have said 'That's it, beat her more, that isn't half enough'. Mary was put to bed one night and the following morning her hands were tied behind her to the bedpost by her stepmother who left her with no food. She was left that way all day and was only untied when it was time for bed. She was then tied up for a further four days until she was able to escape. All she had to eat was a piece of bread the size of her hand. Her father knew of this treatment and also beat her with a strap.

When taken into the care of the police, all she had on was a 'frock' and a 'chemise' and two pieces of rags for stockings. Mary was examined by Doctor Boulton who said there were marks of severe whipping along her shoulders and back and deep old scabs elsewhere on her body. Her right hand was also swollen and she was debilitated for want of food and was too weak to take any.

The father was committed to trial and the step mother fined three pounds plus costs. Mary was taken into custody by the relieving officer.

Rose Taylor

Rose was the daughter of a sweep and lived on the Sow Hill, Pontypool. In January 1869, aged 9, she was charged with attempting to rob the till in the shop of Henry Fox, hairdresser of Pontypool.

Mr Fox stated his till had been repeatedly robbed since the election and he had seen Rose several times in his shop. At last he made a contrivance by means of which a bell rang when anyone touched the till. One Monday, the bell rang and on running upstairs he found Rose just leaving the shop.

Mrs Taylor said she never saw more than a halfpenny or a penny in her daughter's possession and knew nothing of her stealing.

Mr Evans, the judge, in a kind manner pointed out the consequences of crime and bound her over to receive sentence when called upon.

Baby Tanner

A terrible story appeared in the Pontypool Free Press on 29 May 1869. Mr W H Brewer conducted an inquiry at the King's Arms in Newport concerning the death of the illegitimate child of Ann Tanner. The baby was found with its head almost severed from its body.

Elizabeth Millard, who lived in Castle Street, Pill, said she acted as a midwife and on the 18th of May was sent for to go to the house of William Lehay who kept the British Flag in Castle Street. She went to the house and in the bedroom, sitting on a chair was Ann. Elizabeth said to her, 'My girl, what is the matter?'. Ann did not answer but Mrs Lehay said, 'Oh dear, she has been confined and has done something with her child'.

Elizabeth told Ann to show her where the baby was or she would get a policeman. There was a little closet on top of the stairs and the girl went along with her to it and picked up the baby by one arm and gave it to her. Elizabeth then said, 'What have you done to this child? You have cut its throat'. Ann did not make any answer so Elizabeth then said, 'If you don't tell me I will send for a doctor'. It was then Ann replied, 'I did not cut it with a knife, but I did it with my fingernails'. Elizabeth told the girl she would send for the doctor before she touched the child. The baby was then dead. Elizabeth looked at the cut and told Ann that it must have been done with a razor or a knife. Ann though replied and said that she did not touch it with a knife or a razor'. Elizabeth noticed that there was not much blood on the child when she saw it and it was quite warm, therefore Ann could not have been confined for long when she first saw the child. She knew of no clothing having been prepared for the child and she was not engaged by Ann as midwife.

Hannah Morgan, a young girl in service with Ann at the British Flag said that about eleven o clock at night, Ann complained of having a pain in her stomach and said that if she had hot water to bathe her feet, it would do her good. She went downstairs and took up a bucket of hot water which Hannah saw later, it having the appearance of blood having been put in it.

Margaret Lehay, Ann's mistress was examined and owing to the manner in which she gave evidence was threatened by the coroner to be locked up for the night as it was evident that she was not telling all that she knew. Although she was mother of several children she saw nothing in Ann's appearance to excite her suspicions until she saw her at the water tap washing her hands.

Mr David Lewis, surgeon, said he had made a postmortem examination of the body and found a gash across the baby's throat which had completely severed the wind pipe and caused the death of the child. He also stated that the baby had been born alive.

Superintendent Huxtable said a knife was found in the chimney but Dr. Lewis said it was not sharp enough to have made such a wound. The jury returned a verdict of wilful murder against Ann.

At her sentencing in August 1869, Dr. Lewis gave evidence to say that the baby had been born alive but it was impossible to say whether it had had a separate existence. He was of the opinion death was caused by some sharp instrument and not as Ann had alleged, with her finger nails during delivery. The charge of murder therefore, could not be applied to Ann as it was impossible to say whether it had existed separately.

Under these circumstances the judge directed the jury to discard the question of murder and deal with the offence of concealment of birth. After a few minutes the jury found Ann guilty of this lesser offence. In sentencing the judge said -

"I have no doubt that what the surgeon says is true. I have no doubt you inflicted that wound and I am quite of the opinion that the jury with the evidence of the surgeon before them are justified in saying that they cannot see that it was done before the child was separated from the body, therefore they have acquitted you of the murder of the child. You are guilty of concealment of birth and I am bound to treat it as being a bad case of the kind as can be found. The law says that the utmost punishment I can give is that of two years imprisonment with hard labour and I am bound to inflict that upon you.

Mary Ann Morgan

Stories of children being burned by accident were very common. In July 1870, Mr W H Brewer, coroner, held an inquest at the Carpenter's Arms, Cwm Gelly, near Blackwood on the body of Mary Ann. She was just four and a half and had died from injuries received from burning. The jury recorded a verdict to that effect.

Miss Davies

Referred to as only a 'girl' in the Monmouthshire Merlin of May 1872, she was the daughter of David Davies, a miner from Blaenavon. She had a very narrow escape from death one day as a train of laden coal wagons passed by. She climbed up on one of them and after riding a short distance she fell between the couplings and three full trams passed over some parts of her body. She was taken home where Doctor Steel was called in to attend her. The paper reported she was progressing well.

Mrs Davis

Mrs Davis of Newport was the wife of a hairdresser. In June 1872 the Cardiff Times reported on the birth of her twins, the reason being that they were conjoined. The medical man entrusted to her care was Mr Watson. The baby was described in detail by the paper. It had two heads, four arms, three legs, one of which had double bones up to the knee and ten toes. About five hours after birth, one of the twins died. Each child had a perfect central body. At right angles on one side were two legs – right leg of one, left leg of the other. On the opposite side of the body was the leg having ten toes. When the one child died it was perceptible only one half of the leg in question became rigid, that belonging to the body of the dead child. About six hours after what was regarded as death, imperfect respiration again commenced. About twenty four hours later the other twin died but about a quarter of an hour before death the child who had died first, became convulsed. A post postmortem was carried out and it was found the internal organs were natural except for the livers which were joined. In other respects both babies were strong and healthy but natural functions could not be performed.

A photographer, Mr Villers took a photo of the babies and a full report was to appear in medical journals. Many medical men were of the opinion that the occurrence was due to the exhibition of the two headed nightingale in Newport!

Sarah Ann Davies

In July 1872, Mr D Batt held an inquest at the Rising Sun Inn, Blaenavon on Sarah's body. She was two and a half years old and the daughter of a green grocer living in Broad Street. It appeared that she received a slight kick from a horse a short time previous but it seemed no one took any notice of it. The mother left Sarah in the care of a niece one day in order to go to market. On her return, about two in the afternoon, Sarah was found dead in bed. She seemed to have died a natural death and the jury returned a verdict of 'found dead in bed'.

Miss Payne

In September 1872, a terrible case of cruelty to a girl was heard at Pontypool police court. A brick maker named Payne decided his daughter was not as good as she ought to be, so he decided that if she was put in chains and driven, as convicts were driven, she might be better. He fastened a heavy chain, linked together with handcuffs, then bound it around her neck. She was just able to shuffle along and was driven by him to carry water. It was unclear how long he had been doing this but he was sentenced to six months.

Rosanna Harrison

At the Town Hall in Pontypool in November 1872 an inquest was held as to the death of Rosanna. She was aged just seven weeks and was the illegitimate child of a tramping woman. The woman said the child had died in her arms in the street. Dr Williams described Rosanna's condition as much diseased and the jury concluded he death had been from natural causes.

Mrs Stephens

In June 1873, Mrs Stephens of Usk Side Works, gave birth to triplets. All three children lived for only a few hours. The Cardiff Times recorded Mrs Stephens was 'a fair way to convalescence'.

Train Journey

No names were recorded in the South Wales Daily News for this account but it is worth recording to show just how dangerous a train journey could be. One Saturday in November 1873 as the train for Newport on the Brecon and Merthyr line was approaching Church Station, Machen, two young children fell from a carriage doorway, falling violently on to the road. The mother immediately took a perilous jump after them. Fortunately the train was going slowly. All three were taken to Bassaleg Station to receive medical attention. The children were seriously injured, the mother not so much.

Sarah Brook

Mr E D Pratt held an inquest on the body of Sarah from Abergavenny in June 1874. Her mother had gone to bed for a nap and left Sarah, aged five, downstairs by herself. It was thought that she climbed on to the guard in front of the fire to reach some biscuits out of a cupboard when the guard gave way and she fell against the fire which ignited her clothes. Sarah was so severely burned before assistance came, she died a few hours later.

Maria Davis

In September 1874, Thomas Thomas, appeared in Pontypool police court charged with being the father of Maria's illegitimate child. As there was no evidence the case was dismissed. This wasn't the end of the story though as once outside on the street, Maria was accosted by a married woman from the Varteg who said she had three children of her own but all were dead and if Maria agreed she would adopt the 'fatherless bairn'. Maria it seems was glad of the offer. The Monmouthshire Merlin recorded the pair went to a lawyers office to have the bargain ratified and as the mother was later seen about town minus her child, the transfer must have been a success.

Elizabeth Ann Powell

Mrs Thompson of Griffithstown found a little child wandering around near Coed y Gric in May 1875. She took the child to the police station and the following day the child was claimed.

The mother was Elizabeth Powell, she had left the workhouse in Abbeydore, Herefordshire with two illegitimate children, one an infant, the other the Monmouthshire Merlin described as the 'waif she claimed'. Elizabeth had got to Llanvihangle near Abergavenny and met a man named William Thomas who told her he was going to Cwmbran to look for work. He persuaded her to go with him. They arrived at Pontypool Road Station at nine thirty at night and all went and slept under a rick in Coed y Gric. Elizabeth woke at four the following morning and found the man had gone. She also discovered the child had wandered off. Elizabeth went to Cwmbran and told the police who advised her to return to Pontypool but instead of making inquiries at the police station there, she went to a lodging house in Trosnant. Police Sergeant Young in Pontypool then received news from Cwmbran and sent Police Constable Matthews to find her where she was reunited with her child.

Sarah Powell

Sarah was eleven years old in October 1875. Her father was James Powell, a breaksman on the incline, from Abersychan. Sarah was buried at Noddfa Chapel along with her brothers, Thomas aged nine, Lewis aged seven and George, aged four. All had died the same week from fever although their doctor, Dr. Mulligan had done everything he could to save them. On the same night they were buried, another child belonging to the family died also. There was an eldest son, who was at another house at the time, but was so ill he could not attend the funeral. The deaths were attributed to the ground around the house being saturated with sewage.

May Ann Prosser

Described only as a 'little girl', Mary was charged with stealing goods from several people and appeared in court to be sentenced. The bench considered that the parents had shown great neglect in the training of their child and if she were to appear in court at a future time they would send her to a reformatory school. She was sentenced to two months hard labour.

Hannah Bevan

On the 12th January 1877, before Mr James and Mr Llewellyn, Joseph Brimble, a collier, was summoned by Hannah Bevan, a single woman residing at Fleur de Lis and the mother of seven children, to show cause. An order for three shillings a weeks with costs was made.

Rachel Steele

Rachel was sixteen in 1878 and lived in Ebbw Vale. She was crossing one of the Ebbw Vale Company's lines when an engine came along and knocked her down cutting both her legs off just below the knee. She was at once taken home and attended to by Dr. Sheehy, Dr. Davies and their assistant who immediately amputated both legs. She died the following day. An inquest was held in the Victoria Wine Vaults Hotel where a verdict of accidental death was recorded.

Emma Bartlett

Emma was described as a 'young girl' in the Pontypool Free Press of 14 June 1879. She had been before the magistrates several times and been convicted of larceny. A few days previous to the 14th she had been discharged after being locked up for stealing six and a half pence from a child. She was now being charged with stealing a saucepan and scrubbing brush, the property of Edwin Simmons of Talywain. The articles had been stolen from his house and Emma was found offering to sell them to Matilda Griffins. She denied the charge but was put on remand.

Ethel Brewer

An inquest was held by Mr Brewer in September 1879, on the body of Ethel, aged three, who died from the effects of drinking brandy and also toothache mixture. She had managed to get hold of the bottles, drank the contents and died from convulsions. The jury returned a verdict to that effect.

Emily Wilkins

At the fortnightly meeting of the Abergavenny Board of Guardians in March 1881 , it was noted that there had been an increase in the number of young girls from Blaenavon with illegitimate babies seeking help. Emily was one of those girls. The Pontypool Free Press recorded her appearance as being 'smart' with a child in arms, who when asked her age replied 'just twenty'. She asked the clerk if she could come into the house. The clerk asked 'Are you married', to which she replied, 'No Sir'. The clerk then asked, 'How old is the child' – 'thirteen months sir'.

In answer to further questions she revealed she had not affiliated the child, the father had run away. One of her other lovers was John Parry, plate layer. Emma's father accompanied her and explained that as he had a large family already he could not keep her. He described her as 'wayward'. Emma was subsequently accepted into the workhouse and sent to the receiving ward.

A. Ashman

A popular entertainment was given at Zion Hill Baptist Chapel. Miss A Ashman, who took the prize at the Eisteddfod at Pontypool Town Hall played a pianoforte solo called 'The Ash Grove'. Her playing was recorded in the Pontypool Free Press of 27 January 1882 as being 'under good training, her age being eleven'.

Blackwood

In March 1882, the body of a female child was found in the Sirhowy River by Mark Hughes, between the Rock and Fountain and River Row. She was wrapped in an 'old linsey garment" with a new sleeve in it'. An inquest was to be held.

Bridget McCarthy

At the age of 11, in December 1883, Bridget was charged at Pontypool police court with stealing thirty six newspapers, the property of Ishmael Morgan, newsagent of Blaenavon. The offence was admitted. Superintendent Whitfield informed the court that Bridget was greatly neglected at home, had been in trouble before and he believed that it was her father who was encouraging her to steal. Two of McCarthy's other children had also been convicted of theft and both the man and his wife were known to the police as dissipated characters. The chairman, Lieutenant Colonel Byrde told the father, who was stated to be a labourer at the blast furnaces and whose head was bandaged up, he having met with an accident nine weeks previous, that the bench had decided to make an application to send Bridget to an industrial school at Salisbury and would order him to contribute one shilling a week towards her maintenance.

Zilla Deborah Rowlands

On the 27th April, 1884, a Sunday afternoon, Zilla just 8 years old, from Lower Mill, Panteg was subjected to a terrifying assault while picking flowers in a field near Pontypool Road Station. Her attacker was James Probert, aged 21 who was indicted for 'ravishing and carnally knowing' her.

The Monmouthshire Merlin described Zilla as a 'delicate and under-sized child' who went out to play in a field a short distance from her parents home. While she was there she met Probert whom she had previously known. He threw her down and committed the offence with which he was charged. While this assault was taking place, another child, Zilla's friend, Agnes Thomas, was also in the field and witness to the whole event. She was though, too young to do anything about it. After the attack Probert promised to give Zilla a halfpenny at the end of the week. Zilla returned home and told her mother what had happened and was later examined by Mr Essex, a surgeon, who gave evidence to the effect that the offence had been fully committed.

Probert was found guilty and sentenced to ten years penal servitude.

Temperance Williams

Just how perilous childbirth could be can be seen in this next account. In May 1884, Mr E D Batt held two inquests at the police station in Trelleck regarding the death of Temperance Williams, who died on April 28th 1884 and of her illegitimate child which was born on April 22nd and died on April 26th. Temperance died at Penyvan and had been attended two hours before her death by Dr George Mayou of Monmouth and Mr T G Prosser, M R C S., also of Monmouth. Verdicts of death by natural causes were returned for both.

Clara Gooder

At Pontypool petty sessions in January 1885, Clara, aged 14 was charged with stealing from a little girl, the daughter of David James, grocer. She took the money from the child on her way to school. She had a previous conviction and so was sent to prison for one month to be followed by four years at a reformatory.

Annie Gillard

On 11th July 1889, the South Wales Echo reported that Annie from Two Locks, Cwmbran was missing. She was aged 5 and had been left with a neighbour while her mother went to Bassalleg. Annie heard where her mother had gone and instead of going to school as she was supposed to, went off to find her but went missing. The police were called search parties were formed and the canal was dragged but there was no sign.

On 13th July the Cardiff Times recorded her fate. Annie was found dead in Pentre Wood and it was supposed she had lost her way as there was no evidence of foul play, her death being brought about by exposure and want of food.

Mrs Stephens

In November 1892, Mrs Stephens, wife of a Great Western Railway driver from Griffithstown gave birth to triplets two boys and a girl, and all were doing well!

Miss E C Tysoe

In November 1892, the University College of North Wales, Bangor (Flintshire and Denbighshire Dairy Institute) published its examiners reports. The annual examinations had taken place on October 24th, 25th and 26th. All candidates were female and Miss Tysoe of Langstone House, Broadstone, Tintern gained the standard of a pass in the practical examination of butter making.

Baby Moore

Mr C Dauncy, deputy coroner held an inquest at the police station in Blaenavon in 1892 respecting the death of the baby daughter of the Moore's of Bryn Terrace. The first witness examined was Mrs Rogers who stated that the parents of the child lodged with her. The baby when born had appeared to be quite healthy but she would not take breast milk and so was fed with gruel. Mrs Rogers saw the baby the following day but noticed she seemed to be in a dying state and frothing at the mouth. She took her downstairs and nursed her by the fire but within a few minutes the baby died. Mr Moore was questioned by the coroner as to how the baby was wrapped and if the mouth and nose had been covered preventing proper breathing. The inquest was adjourned for a short time as the coroner was not satisfied with the evidence. A doctor was summoned who had seen the baby when alive and he stated she had seemed fine and attributed death to suffocation due to being too wrapped up. This verdict was recorded.

Ada Meredith

This account goes to show just how dangerous measles was to a child. An inquest was held in May 1892 at Pontypool Town Hall as to the death of Ada who was 11 months old. She was the daughter of Charles Meredith of 33 High Street. Mrs Meredith said Ada had been unwell having contracted measles and had subsequently died. Dr S B Mason said he had attended Ada since the beginning of March for measles and bronchitis. His last visit was on March 19th when Ada was convalescing. He had examined her body and found no marks of any violence and from what the mother had told him he stated Ada had died from convulsions. Dr Mason declared Mrs Meredith was a very good mother and very careful with her children. A verdict of death from natural causes was returned.

Isabella Driver

It was June 1893 when Sydney Meredith, a 17 year old farm labourer from Penallt near Monmouth was charged with assaulting Isabella, aged 10. She lived in Llantarnam and was going to the railway station to meet her father when she was accosted by Meredith, who kissed her, put his arm around her waist and behaved indecently. Luckily the mother came up at the same time and prevented anything further from happening. The father afterwards appeared on the scene and gave him a severe thrashing. Meredith ran into the river to escape the irate parent. When he was arrested by Officer Keylock his clothes were wet and his nose bleeding. Meredith, whose face still showed marks of the blows given by the father, admitted Isabella's story was true. As it was a first offence he was fined twenty shillings or fourteen days in prison.

Alice May Ellis

Mr Lyndon Moore related a sad story to Newport County magistrates in September 1906 concerning David Hughes, a labourer from Henllys who was charged by the NSPCC with child neglect.

Mr Moore began by reminding the jury that Mrs Hughes had drowned the previous May, while trying to save her child from drowning. As a result, neighbours had rallied round, made a collection and bought clothes for the children and for Mr Hughes. However most of these were pawed by him in order to buy drink.

Mrs Hughes had one child from a previous marriage, Alice, and

Mr Hughes was exceptionally cruel to her. He was not bound to keep her but he did, it suited him to do so as she acted as housekeeper. Mr Moore stated the children were fed on boiled bread, pepper and salt and Mr Hughes threatened to cut their throats if they asked for more. Alice stated that the other children were not treated as badly as her, however when someone told Mr Hughes that the little boy was crying he came home and 'beat the boy shocking'. Mr Hughes had also threatened to cut Alice's throat and to murder her for asking for food to feed her brothers and sisters. The children also cried for food to which he threatened to cut their heads off.

Mrs Beynon, Southwood and Cousins, neighbours, gave evidence that the baby was left with no milk for nine hours, that the children had dry bread for breakfast and nothing more all day other than what was given by neighbours. Inspector Sparkes said that Mr Hughes was a 'drunken loafer and if it wasn't for the neighbours, the children would have starved'.

Mr Hughes's defence was that he lost himself to drink after his wife died. He was sentenced to four moths hard labour. The children were sent to the workhouse until a new home could be found for them.

Unknown Baby

Mr M Roberts Jones conducted an inquiry in Cwmbran in April 1907 into the death of an unknown female infant whose body was found in the Afon Llwyd at Llantarnam.

P C Hughes stated that he found the body on a small island in the river opposite Llantarnam Abbey. Dr W Murphy made a post mortem examination and stated that the body was that of a healthy child and that life must have existed for about seven days. There were no signs of violence but the right side of the lower jaw had been eaten by rats or crows. There was nothing to show the child was alive when put into the water. The coroner suggested the child was possibly illegitimate and might have been thrown out of a passing train into the river! An open verdict was recorded.

Mrs Twissel

Mr M Roberts Jones conducted another inquest in Cwmbran in July 1910 on the infant daughter of Mr and Mrs Twissel of Ventnor

Road.

Susan Jane Pranglen, neighbour, stated that at three o clock on a Friday morning that month, she had heard shouting and screaming and on going into the back yard saw Mrs Twissel, who was trying to attract the attention of her husband. A midwife was sent for and when she returned she saw a baby had been born. She at once sent for the police as the child was dead.

Dr Murphy stated that he saw the child and she had had a separate existence. She was fully developed and healthy. In answer to the coroner, the doctor said that if the child had been properly attended to at birth, she would have lived. A verdict of accidental suffocation through want of attention at birth was returned.

Hannah Maria Styles

In January 1916 an inquest was held in Abergavenny on a storm fatality in Blaenavon. Hannah was thirteen years old, the daughter of William, a collier of Old Pwlldu. Evidence showed that during the storm she was told by a roadman, John Champion, to walk behind a cart which was going along the Abergavenny road, in order to protect her from the wind and prevent her from being blown into the brickworks pond. At that moment, a horse attached to a grocer's cart which had been frightened by the wind, bolted down the road and immediately after it had passed Hannah was found on the ground, bleeding from a severe wound in her neck. It was assumed she looked out from behind the cart and was struck by the cart drawn by the runaway horse. The jury returned a verdict of accidental death and exonerated the driver of the grocer's cart from any blame.

MARRIAGE

Miss Lamb

Unfortunately Miss Lamb's Christian name was not recorded when the occasion of her marriage was reported by the Monmouthshire Merlin in January 1851. She was though, the daughter of David Lamb and she married Henry Motonnier Hawkins of Tredunnock.

These were the times when marriages of the wealthy could involve the whole community. The local chapel was dense with spectators, amongst them some of the major families in the county. The bride wore a white figured satin dress and the Merlin recorded a 'gracefulness in her movements and a calmness in her demeanor'. Once she had given her hand in marriage the church bells of St Mary's rang out and the sound of cannon fire was heard. On leaving the chapel, they alighted the groom's carriage pulled by four horses and proceeded to Mr Lamb's house, followed by other carriages.

Mr and Mrs Hawkins left about two o clock in the afternoon amid cheers from the inhabitants of the area to spend their honeymoon in Paris.

Mr Hawkins, highly respected in the neighbourhood and considered a kind and generous man, remembered the poor and donated meals of roast beef and plum pudding to occupants of the almshouses and distributed money to the poor of the town along with coal, blankets and clothing. In the evening, tenantry and friends gathered at Great House Farm where the night was spent in celebration.

Miss Lewis

The whole of Risca was the scene of a general holiday for the marriage of Miss Lewis in April 1855. She was the daughter of D Lewis who was related to John and Thomas Lewis, proprietors of tin works in the area. She married George Banks of the Pontymister Works.

From an early hour groups of people, who had been given the day off from the works, set about building triumphal arches at different locations throughout the village. Many flags and banners also flew and cannon were placed at the foundry and other places. A band added music to the preparations. Parties wearing white rosettes and wedding favours were seen all around. The train drivers placed evergreens and flowers on their carriages.

The ceremony was performed at Risca Church by the Reverend David Davis. On leaving the church the pair found the path covered in flowers while cheers from assembled crowds greeted them. Nine carriages transported the party to the wedding breakfast where after a series of toasts the couple left for Cheltenham and London.

Later, forty of the agents of the works were invited to carry on celebrating at dinner at the Albert Inn. The workmen and their wives and children were also not forgotten, the large rooms of the Pontymister and Risca Works were used for a party where a wedding cake of almost the diameter of a railway turntable was distributed and feasted upon.

Isabella Arkley

A number of the inhabitants of Christchurch, near Newport witnessed the marriage of Isabella to William F Willmott in August 1855. The church and paths leading up to it, were decorated with flowers and evergreens. Afterwards, children in connection with the church were invited for tea and cake, after which they gave three cheers for the bride and groom and for the rest of the family.

Miss Watkins

Miss Watkins married the Reverend William James on Tuesday 28th July 1863. The Reverend Lewis Edwards performed the ceremony at Lord Llanover's Welsh Church in Abercarn. It was conducted in Welsh and a Welsh bible was presented to the bride as she stepped from her carriage by Miss Matthews on behalf of the Welsh Church. The bride, groom and wedding party then left for Abercarn Uchaf, one of the residences of Lord Llanover. The feast was conducted on temperance principles by the absence of all fermented liquors which were disused by members of the Welsh Presbyterian Church generally. The inhabitants of the area showed their respect with triumphal arches, festoons and banners.

Miss Tobias

Argoed was the scene of excitement in April 1866 as a consequence of the marriage of Miss Tobias to Mr Daniel Walters of Castle Inn. Mr Walters family had connections to the area for generations and they were highly respected in the area. Many neighbours took interest in the celebration. Church bells rang and the bride and groom were greeted with a triumphal arch, flags, the firing of guns and deafening cheers

Miss Brewer

In June 1870, the wedding of Miss Brewer of Machen, the youngest daughter of John Brewer of Bovill House and bridegroom Arthur McCloughry of Ross, Herefordshire, took place. The church was profusely decorated with flowers. The bride wore a white silk dress with blue stripe and lace trimmings and orange blossoms. Mr S J Brewer was the best man. A brisk firing of cannon was heard as the party left the church and was kept up at intervals during the day. The couple left in the afternoon for a wedding tour.

Miss Bevan

It was a Monday morning in June 1878 when the marriage took place of Miss Bevan, only daughter of the esteemed townsman,

Arnold Bevan to Mr Edwin Southwood Jones of Henllys House, Cwmbran, manager of Messrs C Hill and company's Henllys Colliery. The ceremony was performed at Trevethin Church by Reverend J C Llewellin. The bride wore her travelling dress and was given away by her father. She was also accompanied by her mother and brothers. The groom was accompanied by his father, Mr Jones of Derby. The ceremony was witnessed by many persons, mostly young ladies. Mrs A A Williams played the organ as the party advanced to the altar and Mendelssohn's Grand Wedding March as the bride and groom passed down the aisle from the vestry.

On returning from church to the house of Mr Bevan, breakfast was prepared. Groups of people gathered on the streets to see the horse drawn carriages rush past. Afterwards the bride and groom travelled to London, then to Paris and on to the Rhine.

Miss Potter

On a Thursday morning in September 1879, there was much excitement in Pontypool owing to the marriage of Miss Potter to Mr Charles Davis. The marriage took place at eight in the morning at Trevethin Church. The members of St James's Church choir attended and took part in the service as the bride and groom were also members. The Reverend J.C. Llewellyn performed the ceremony. The bride wore a dress of fawn coloured silk, trimmed with blue and a matching hat. Miss Davis, sister of the groom was bridesmaid and Mr Tom Davis, brother of the groom was best man. The first hymn was sung by the choir as the bride entered the church - hymn number 241 – 'The Voice that breathed o'er Eden, That earliest wedding morn'.

Mendelssohn's Wedding March played as they left the church and outside quantities of rice were thrown over them and into their carriage. Wreaths of evergreens with flags were stretched across Albion Road, near Glannant Cottage, Miss Potter's residence and salutes were fired by men employed by Mr John Moseley, also a member of the choir.

Florence Lawrence

Florence was the daughter of David Lawrence of Llangibby Castle. In February 1880, she married Mr Arthur Evans, son of W.

Evans, J.P. The whole village of Llangibby was decorated for the occasion, arches of evergreens stretched across roads with flags and banners bearing good wishes from the inhabitants. In and around the church, decorating had been carried out and a scarlet cloth had been laid at the entrance and through the porch. The church was filled with spectators. At 11.30 a.m. the bride arrived in her carriage and she entered the church with her father followed by eight bridesmaids. Each wore ivory Dacca silk trimmed with Brussels lace, a mob cap with spring flowers and each carried an ivory and lace fan, presented by the groom.

On leaving, the bride and groom were sprinkled with rice and the organ played the Wedding March. Guns were fired at the castle and a wedding breakfast was prepared in the Great Hall. The pair later left for their honeymoon in the south of England. Festivities though carried on at the castle into the evening. The bride's presents were displayed in the drawing room.

Miss Matthews

On a Monday morning in November 1883 at Mynyddislwyn Parish Church, Miss Matthews, only daughter of Mr D L Matthews, Crown Hotel, Abercarn married Mr J Green, mining engineer, Celynen Colliery. The ceremony was performed by Rev J Griffiths. The bride wore a fawn satin dress, trimmed with plush and a hat. After the wedding breakfast the couple left on the midday train for Bournemouth. Several pieces of music were played for the occasion by the Celynen String Band.

Rachel Hay

Rachel, of Ivy House, Usk, was the second daughter of Mr C Hay of Newport. She married David Howell, a merchant, also from Newport in the parish church in Usk in May 1885. The Reverend S Baker performed the ceremony and the bride wore a cream satin dress trimmed with lace and a veil crowned by a wreath of orange blossoms. She was given away by her brother, C J Hay. The bridesmaids wore cream and blue satin trimmed with lace. Afterwards a party was held at Ivy House where the bride received a large number of 'costly' presents.

Gladys Elizabeth Mitchell

Gladys was the elder daughter of F J Mitchell of Llanfrechfa Grange. Her marriage took place to Major Cleeve in January 1894 at Llanfrechfa Church. The bride wore white satin embroidered with pearls, a veil of Honiton lace, ornaments, diamonds and carried a bouquet of lilies of the valley. There were twelve bridesmaids dressed in Bengaline silk with bouquets of narcissi. The ceremony was performed by the Reverend C W Tyler of Leeds parish church. There was a choral service and an organist played the Wedding March as the party left the church. They then passed between a company of the Mountain Mule battery from Newport Barracks who presented arms. On arriving back at Llanfrechfa Grange, cannon fired from within the grounds and Cwmbran Brass Band played on the lawn in front of the house during the wedding breakfast. Lord Llangattock proposed a toast and the bridegroom revealed he and his bride were going to a distant land and were sure of a good reception. The wedding presents were numerable and valuable. The honeymoon was spent in Cornwall.

Francis Mary Powell

At All Saints Church, Llanfrechfa in October 1902, a large congregation gathered to witness the marriage of Francis to Rowland Hill. The Reverend T Reynolds officiated and the bride was given away by her father, William. She wore a dress of grey silk voile with white and silk passementerie trimming and a white hat with grey and steel trimmings. Her bouquet was flowers and ferns. The two bridesmaids wore cream dresses with nuns veiling trimmed with cream silk and cream hats. The reception was at the residence of the bride's father and her travelling dress was grey beaver.

Margaret Haig-Thomas

In July 1908 in Christchurch, near Newport, Margaret, the only daughter of Mr D A Thomas M.P. And Mrs Thomas of Llanwern Park married Captain Humphrey Mackworth, the eldest surviving son of Colonel Sir Arthur Mackworth and Lady Mackworth of Caerleon Priory.
The bride was given away by her father. There were no

bridesmaids, their places being taken by little Miss Mary Conway Gordon and Master Rodolf Haig dressed in King Charles costumes of white satin. A large number of the Llangibby Hunt, of which the groom was the master attended and among the presents was a large number of hunting articles. The bride's parents gave her a cheque, a dressing case and a rope of pearls. The reception party was held at Llanwern Park and the honeymoon in Norway.

Bernice Develin

An Irish wedding took place at St Luke's Church, Pontnewynydd on 29th March 1910 between Miss Bernice Grace Lydia Miriam Develin, formerly of Dublin and Mr Frederick George Davies of Abergavenny. The bride wore a white silk empire gown with Irish lace, silver trimmings and wreath with a veil of real Brussels net. She carried a bouquet of white hyacinths, lily of the valley, orchids and roses. Three of her sisters were bridesmaids. Miss C, wore heliotrope silk and hat trimmed to match while the Misses D and E wore hand painted princess robes and large white hats with blue flowers and carried shillelaghs decorated with bunches of shamrock tied with green ribbons. The presents were numerable and valuable, including a silver tea and coffee service and a black marble clock presented by the staff of Abergavenny Steam Laundry of which the bride is manageress. The reception took place at Rathgar, St Luke's Road, Pontnewynydd, the residence of her parents. After the ceremony the bridal party together with the vicar were photographed.

Early Marriage Customs

Early newspapers mostly concerned themselves with the weddings of the wealthy of society, but what of working class women? In 1859, the Monmouthshire Merlin answers this question with an article on marriage customs in Wales -

"Very little is known by the public generally about the manners and customs of the Welsh, among the lower orders of whom there still lingers much of that brotherhood which characterised our ancestors several centuries ago. One of their most curious practices is 'bidding' which is invariably followed in the agricultural districts. As soon as the wedding day is fixed, the contracting parties print and distribute small hand-bills of which the following is a specimen :-

'As we intend entering the matrimonial state we are encouraged by our friends and relations to make a bidding on the occasion, which will be held on Friday July 10th, 1859, at the house called Clyndrinog, borough of Loughhor when and where the favour of your good and agreeable company is humbly solicited; and whatever donation you may be pleased to bestow on us then will be thankfully received, and cheerfully repaid whenever called for on a similar occasion. Your humble servants – David Williams, Elizabeth Davies.

The young man's mother and the young woman's father and mother desire that all debts of the above nature due to them be paid on the above day.'

The number of persons who assemble on such occasions varies according to the character and connection of the parties interested. Both issue billets to their acquaintances; and thus there are frequently congregated as many as one hundred or one hundred and eighty individuals of both sexes and all ages. Should the bride and bridegroom live some distance apart, their respective retinues set out early in the morning, headed by a fiddler, whose native music enlivens the journey. They generally contrive to make a halfway meeting where both parties amalgamate and proceed directly to the church. On the way it is customary for some of the neighbouring lads to hide behind a tree or hedge, and suddenly fire a salute, much to the consternation of the females in the joyous procession.

After the ceremony is over, the whole assemblage repair to the house of the bridegroom's father to partake of some refreshment (for which each pays his or her quota), and to deposit their donations. The amount collected varies according to the circumstances of the individuals, averaging from £30 to £40. In some instances it has reached £150. The sum thus gained affords to the young beginners considerable assistance, enabling them to commence life free and unembarrassed by pecuniary difficulties. As will be seen by the printed invitation, the individuals thus assisted hold themselves responsible, in point of honour, for the repayment of the various sums contributed, when those who advance them are about to take a similar step. Should those who make donations not require repayment on their own account, they have the power of demanding it in favour of any of their children. In almost every case there are a number of bachelor and maiden contributors; and thus the newly-wedded couple are on the whole, gainers; while the repayments also fall due at distant and scattered periods.

As at the old Scotch penny weddings, the proceedings are wound up with a dance in the barn or other convenient apartment, where with music, dancing and drinking the mirth soon grows loud and furious; - fortunate if it terminates as harmless as it began."

These were weddings on a budget, and if following the Scottish tradition, guests brought their own food and drink too. The emphasis for the poor was not on the day itself, but having a good start to married life.

HOME LIFE

The marriages of the ordinary working class women may not have been recorded by Victorian newspapers but many aspects of their home lives were.

Mary Murphy

Mary was charged with assaulting Catherine Edwards on 12th February 1856. Catherine stated that on the day in question there was an argument about the oven, which was in use among the inhabitants of the neighbourhood of Pontypool and which had been engaged by both in the usual way, namely by putting a piece of coal inside it. During the dispute, Mary struck Catherine in the face, giving her a black eye and causing her nose to bleed.

Witnesses Eliza Creese and Bridget Bell declared they had each seen the blow given. Anther witness, Hannah Carey was called who claimed it was Mary's turn to use the oven and Catherine had no right to occupy it. There was enough room in the oven to bake bread for three families but Catherine wanted to have it all to herself.

Margaret Harris said she saw the affray right from the start and swore it was Catherine who struck Mary first and shoved her several times before she hit back. The case was dismissed and Catherine was ordered to pay thirteen shillings and sixpence costs.

Ellen Phillips

William Watkins, a young man of eighteen, employed at Newport Docks was judged to be the father of Ellen's illegitimate child. Ellen had a 'respectable' appearance and was formerly a servant at the Westgate Hotel. It appeared that William had promised to marry her. She had been giving him money to assist with buying furniture though none appeared to have been bought. The Bench decided it was a case of seduction and ordered him to pay five shillings a week for the first six weeks and two shillings and six pence afterwards as well as the costs of the confinement and court costs. The court then recommended he make friends with Ellen and marry her.

Mary Ann Jenkins

Mary, of Springvale in Cwmbran, attempted to commit suicide by throwing herself in the canal near the Cwmbran furnaces. A man named John Jones happened to be in the area and succeeded in dragging her out. When asked her reason for trying to kill herself she said it was because her husband was an 'irreclaimable drunk'.

Dorothy Price

On December 31st 1857, Dorothy was charged with assaulting Jane Fitzgerald of Garndiffaith in a dispute over an oven. The oven was used by numerous people in the neighbourhood, communal ovens were the norm, but the question was on this occasion who had priority of use. Jane stated that Dorothy had thrown a firebrand at her and also hit her with the handle of a sweeping brush. A witness stated that Jane went to the oven and drew out the fire which had been placed there by Dorothy. This witness lived next door to the oven and swore that no assault had been committed and that Jane was to blame. The case was dismissed and Jane had to pay the costs.

Patience Francis

In October 1861, Patience was in court giving evidence against her husband, William, a farmer in Llangibby. He was charged with using threats against her and their son Thomas, aged 20. They were so afraid of William that they feared living with him. Thomas stated that when his father came down to breakfast on the 20th, a Sunday morning he began to swear at him and his mother, beat him, kick him and tried to stab him with a knife.. William was bound over to keep the peace for six months.

Sarah Phillips

Sarah was described as a 'respectably dressed woman' by the Monmouthshire Merlin in September 1863. She appeared at the Caerleon petty sessions to apply to have her husband bound over to keep the peace. She said that they lived in Cwmbran and had been married for twelve years and during the last three he had been turning to drink. When he was in a drunken state he would beat her, throw knives at her, break household items and threaten to do her harm. Her husband did not deny that he got drunk but did deny having hit her. The magistrates ordered him to find two sureties for ten pounds each and to be bound himself in twenty pounds to keep the peace for six months and to pay the fourteen shillings and sixpence costs.

Julia Llewellin

Julia was charged with assaulting Ann Lewis and John Lewis, Ann's husband, was charged with assaulting Julia. All lived in Cwmbran and in December 1863 an argument ensued over the oven. The parties lived in the same row of houses and in this row was an oven for general use. On one day, both parties wanted to use the oven at the same time. Mrs Llewellin brought out a shovel of fire to put in the oven and John Lewis threw it out of her hand, some of the fire touching Mrs Lewis. A row then took place which resulted in John Lewis giving Julia a black eye and Julia striking Mrs Lewis and her baby. They were all ordered to pay the expenses of seven shillings between them.

Julia Corbett

In the Monmouthshire Merlin of April 1865, we discover the ratio of ovens to houses when Ann Love and Abigail Driscoll were charged with assaulting Julia. The parties all lived in the same row of houses in Cwmbran and there was one oven for every five houses.

The women met at the oven and argued over whose turn it was to use it. The Bench ordered them to pay the costs between them – four shillings each.

Mrs Davies

Mrs Davies of Cwmbran reported her husband to the police in September 1865 resulting in him being brought before the magistrates at Caerleon petty sessions. He was charged with assaulting her and she told the court that for some reason he was jealous of her and when he came home drunk he abused her. On the last occasion he had come home drunk and beat her about the arms and body. That was when she reported him. Her husband pleaded guilty and asked her to forgive him. The Bench bound him over to keep the peace for six months and to pay eleven shillings and sixpence costs.

Mrs George

In October 1867, Mrs George found herself chargeable to the Pontypool workhouse as her husband, James, had deserted her. He was eventually found in Gloucester and apprehended. He had left her to the mercy of the workhouse for twenty five days and it wasn't the first time he had deserted her. He was sent to prison with fourteen days hard labour.

Unknown woman

A young woman, around twenty, from Ebbw Vale had been married for about a year when she eloped with a younger man around nineteen. He had been lodging in the house for three months when the pair packed up a quantity of clothing, some belonging to the husband, before running away together. They were traced by the police to Staffordshire, captured and brought back to James Street station where a large crowd had gathered to follow them to the police station while hurling abuse at them.

Wife Selling

The Monmouthshire Merlin did not record any names for this

following account but it is too good a story to leave out. In October 1870, there was much gossip circulating in Blaenavon about a man who allowed his wife to be sold. Some months earlier, a widow of about 45 and a widower of 60 decided to marry. It is unknown whether the marriage was satisfactory but an old boyfriend of the widow offered her husband five pounds for her. The offer was accepted, the cash was paid and off she went. The whole affair was carried out with good humour by all parties, said the Merlin.

Elizabeth Pullin

Elizabeth was in court in October 1870, though she did not appear. She was charged with assaulting her husband, Robert, a butcher who had a stall in Pontypool Market. For reasons not specified in the Monmouthshire Merlin, she and the children had been in the workhouse but he had taken them out. Elizabeth met him on the road and refused to live with him. An argument began and he stated that Elizabeth had thrown a stone at his head. The case was adjourned. The Bench didn't seem to have a good opinion of him, again for reasons unknown, and requested to see Elizabeth instead. She appeared in court in mid October, without Robert and the case was dismissed.

Mrs Watkins

In January 1877, Mrs Watkins, age twenty six, wife of George Watkins, mysteriously disappeared. George was a timber man at Abercarn colliery and regularly worked nights. One Thursday night in January, Mrs Watkins left for the Pantyresk Inn which was mid way between Abercarn and Mynyddislwyn Parish Church. George, for some reason, did not go to work that night and as it was getting late, decided to go and look for his wife. On his way, he found her in the company of William Marsh, whose parents lived next door to him. George, clearly doubted his wife's fidelity at this point and began to beat her, Marsh having run off.

George then left to return home and on arriving, woke up his neighbours, Mr Marsh senior and wife and informed them both of the events. Mr and Mrs Marsh then set off to find Mrs Watkins whom George said he had left on the spot he found her with their son. William Marsh by this time was home and in bed.

The following afternoon it was reported that Mrs Watkins body had been thrown up by the river near North Risca. Later in the day, a hat, some money and other articles tied in a shawl were found by the side of the Sirhowy River at Pontllanfraith and were recognised as belonging to Mrs Watkins.

William Marsh denied anything untoward had happened with Mrs Watkins. She had been married for ten years and appeared to be happy. There were four children and as the Monmouthshire Merlin recorded

'much sympathy was felt for them and their father, who is a very respectable man'.

Mr W. H. Brewer conducted an inquest and an open verdict of 'Found dead' was returned.

Emma Holder

Emma was the landlady of the Queen Adelaide beer house in Snatchwood, Abersychan. In February 1877, her son Henry, described by the Cardiff Times as a 'powerful-looking young man' appeared at Pontypool police court charged with assaulting her. Henry lived with her and on one night, after a difference of opinion he attacked her and severely kicked her. Dr. Mulligan of Abersychan certified Emma was in a dangerous condition which might turn more serious if inflammation or erysipelas set in. A certificate was therefore presented stating she could not appear at court for a fortnight. Henry was remanded in custody with bail refused.

Mary Jones

Mary's husband was summoned to the petty sessions in September 1879. They lived in Cwmbran and he was accused of threatening her. The court was told that he hit her, pulled the hair out of her head and threatened to cut her throat with a razor. The Bench ordered him to pay four shillings a week for May's maintenance and granted a separation.

Caroline Wilkinson

At Pontypool police court, in April 1887, Caroline made the first application in the district under the Married Woman's Maintenance (in case of desertion) Act of 1886. It called for an order on her husband, who had deserted her to contribute to her support. She told the court they had married in 1880 and had lived together until 1883 when he made an excuse for her to go and visit her sister. When she returned from her visit, he had gone and taken most of their things with him, She had not seen him since. He had sent her a small amount but it wasn't much and she was dependent on her father, a labourer. She had two children but after her husband's disappearance, one of them had died. The Bench made an order for him to contribute five shillings a week and pay the costs.

Mrs Phillips

Mrs Phillips of Abercarn attempted to hang herself in July 1887. Her husband, a haulier, ill treated her so badly that one Saturday it was found necessary to obtain medical treatment. She also obtained a certificate to testify to the injuries in order to assist her in obtaining a separation order. Four days later, on Wednesday, the ill treatment happened again after which she left the house with a rope, saying goodbye to some of the neighbours as she went. She proceeded to a wood behind a chemical works but neighbours saw what she was up to and a butcher named Lewis followed her. He reached her just as she was securing the rope to a tree. Mrs Phillips was brought back and taken to a neighbours house, she was known to be a respectable and hard working woman and much indignation was expressed towards her husband.

Mary Davies

A woman wasn't safe just to open her front door. Mary, a married woman living near the Rising Sun Inn, Blaina, did just that in October 1888. As she did so, the person on the other side, a collier named Joseph Dimmick, used insulting language and threatened to throw her liver out. Then he began to hit her. Witness Elizabeth Jane Davies confirmed what Mary had stated and Joseph was fined one pound or fourteen days in prison.

Mary Townsend

On the night of December 15th 1890, Mary was assaulted by her husband, an ironworker and landlord of the Railway Inn, Cwmbran. She said that her husband was a heavy drinker. He attacked her, hitting her with his fist, in her face, giving her two black eyes. He also threatened to murder her and therefore she was afraid to live with him. The magistrates treated the case as an aggravated assault, fined him forty shillings and granted a separation. He was also ordered to pay ten shillings a week towards his wife's maintenance.

Rosa Ann Williams

When Rosa married her husband David Murrell on October 18th 1892, she probably thought she was his only wife. She wasn't though, he was already married to someone else who was still alive at the time of the marriage. In court in April 1894, the witnesses to the first marriage were not in attendance. The only witness called was Police Constable Keylock who proved the arrest of David, of Oakfield Cwmbran, who was remanded in custody.

Mary Ann Rees

Mary, a mother of four from Abercarn made an attempt to drown herself in August 1894. She was addicted to drink and as a result quarreled with her husband. On the day in question, she left her house determined to end her life. On reaching the canal near the Bush Inn, Abercarn, she deliberately threw herself in but was seen by a man named T. Jones who rescued her. When charged by Police Constable Barter she admitted the offence and expressed a determination to end her life. She was taken into custody and brought up at Abercarn police station who remanded her until September 7th, accepting sureties of five pounds from herself and her husband to ensure her appearance.

Mary Ann Buckley

Mary made an application to Cwmbran magistrates for a separation from her husband, Dennis, a labourer, in February 1899. She did so under the Married Women's Act of 1895. The marriage took place in Pontypool in 1885 but within a year he had left her. Since then he had lived with her off and on but the whole amount of time didn't amount to eighteen months. He never furnished the house, paid any rent and the last time he had lived with her was in January 1894. He had paid her some money under an order obtained from the Board of Guardians but had had several terms in prison for not paying. The separation order was granted with seven shillings and six pence a week maintenance.

Margaret Jeffrey Smith

In a cottage in the Square, Cwmbran, lived Margaret Smith. Her fourth son, James was a boatman who had had charge of a party, three of whom drowned at Tintern. On being questioned about the accident, he told the jury and coroner that his age was sixty eight and it was further discovered, his mother, Margaret had passed her one hundredth birthday and was parent to twenty one children.

He told a newspaper that Margaret had sixteen sons and five daughters. She lived with one of her younger daughters who was aged fifty four. The chief guide to her age was centred on her youngest son. He was born when she was fifty seven. He died at the age of thirty, the other siblings had scattered through the county. In September 1899, when this story was printed, there were only six of Margaret's children left alive.

Margaret also had thirty four grandchildren, thirty four great grandchildren and four great great grandchildren. Margaret's eyesight was beginning to fail but when she had had perfect eyesight she could thread needles and make clothes for her great great grandchildren. Although she was not able to sew in 1899, she could still nurse the little ones, rock them in her chair and tell them stories. Her memory was also failing but physically she was able to walk from her home to Cwmbran and Pontnewydd and in the summer of 1898 she had walked over the mountain to Pontypool returning along the lower road along the canal, a distance of seven or eight miles.

Mary Gladden

On September 29th 1900, Mary was subjected to a violent assault by her husband Charles, aged sixty and employed at the Patent Nut and Bolt Company in Cwmbran. He had hit her on her head with an iron bar in an attempt to kill her. Dr. Marshall of Pontnewydd said he first saw Mary at her home, 3 Spring Street at 8.30 p.m. She was sat in a chair conscious but trembling and had two wounds to her head – one was two and a half inches long and the other an inch long. The longer one was more serious and though he could not see any evidence of a fracture there was a cut through the scalp that had penetrated the bone. Mary suffered severe shock as a result and her husband was remanded in custody on a charge of attempted murder. It was hoped once Mary was better she might be able to give evidence which she did in mid October.

Mary was a middle aged woman who had been married to Charles for seventeen years, he was her third husband. On the night of the assault he had returned home from a drinking session around 9.30. He wanted to go out again but Mary prevented him from going so it was this that caused the attack. He became angry and struck her twice on the back of her head with a poker. Mary added that Charles was a good husband and that they rarely 'had words' The assault was the only time he had hit her. Charles then became very excitable at court and said 'I struck her twice' and that he did not do it intentionally. As Charles had already been in custody for sixteen days he was sentenced to one month in prison and bound over to keep the peace for six.

Elizabeth Williams

At Cwmbran police station in July 1902, Elizabeth applied for a separation order from her husband, Thomas, a labourer in the ironworks. She stated that they were married in 1881 and had ten children, seven of whom were under sixteen. She left Thomas the previous April due to him having an affair with another woman. She went to the workhouse and Thomas came to see her off. His other woman had one of the children with her and Elizabeth stated that the woman took any opportunity to annoy her. Thomas stated that he had no defence to the application and so it was granted by the magistrates. Thomas had to pay thirteen shillings a week though in maintenance and Elizabeth was given custody of all the children under sixteen.

Naomi Christopher

After being married for fourteen years, Naomi of Llandevenny obtained a separation order in 1903, from her husband, a hay cutter on the grounds of aggravated assault. She stated there were no children and during their marriage he had taken to drinking. On the night of the 20th August he had come home very drunk. She was upstairs and so he called out to her. He told her that while he had been out in Magor, someone had told him that a man had been to the house that day. Naomi told him that it wasn't true but he hit her anyway in the face, giving her two black eyes. He then dragged her down the stairs and hit her again. While only dressed in her nightdress he pushed her outside into the rain. The separation order was granted and the husband had to pay costs plus six shillings and sixpence towards his wife's maintenance.

Louisa Collier

In September 1903, Louisa's husband was summoned for persistent cruelty. Louisa said she was married to him on 24th August, 1900. There were no children alive. In recent times he had struck her until her mouth was full of blood. She ran off down the garden but he chased after her, tearing the clothes off her back as he did so. On another occasion he hit her on the arms and between the shoulders. When cross examined, Louisa explained that the fault was with her husband's parents and that she could not live with them. Her husband's response was that she should leave and if she did not do so, he would throw her out of a window. He then stated that he lived with his parents as they had built the house between them. He blamed her family for putting her up to taking out a summons. As Louisa had no witnesses the case was adjourned for all to settle their differences.

Rose Crane

Rose lived in Pontypool and also in September 1903 was in court, her husband having been summoned for cruelty. Rose said that she went into the Prince of Wales Inn on a Saturday night to ask her husband for some money to buy food for herself and children. He gave her a sovereign but she knew he had over two more sovereigns coming to him that week and so she asked him how she was able to keep herself and five children as well as him on that. He told her to go outside with him and he would discuss the matter with her there.

She went with him and he responded by kicking her down the street and hitting her. She then went home and he arrived there a bit later. As he was drunk she tried to avoid him by going back out. But he followed her, up a lane where he kicked her on the leg from the ankle to the thigh until it was bruised all over. Next morning she asked him if he was not ashamed of what he had done but he replied by saying he was not sorry and should have kicked her inside out. She went on to explain he had done no work for a month, and had not attempted to. She had no food in the house for herself or the children. She was a widow when she married him and two of the children were from her previous marriage. These, her present husband refused to keep and told her she must obtain relief from the workhouse. He pleaded guilty and said he was sorry and promised to behave in future. The chairman gave him a lecture on cruelty, advised him to 'go to work and stick to it', and for Rose's sake he would only be bound over to keep the peace and pay costs.

Hannah Coles

Mr W Everett, coroner for South Monmouth held an inquest in the police station, Cwmbran in July 1904 on Hannah, aged 55, the wife of Henry, of 22 Grange Road. She committed suicide by hanging herself to her bedstead. Henry said Hannah was addicted to drink. She had had about a dozen bouts that year each of which lasted for about a fortnight, though she never threatened to harm herself in any way. Hannah was intoxicated and had been drinking all week. He had last seen her alive when leaving for work at 5.30 in the morning. On Henry's return home from work at 7.30 in the evening, he found her, tied from her neck with her apron to the foot of the bed. A lodger, named William Probert also said he found her dead, in a kneeling position, on returning from work. William's wife, Hannah Probert, stated though, that when she had seen her an hour before her death, Hannah appeared to be sober. The jury, after being advised that they could not return a verdict that death was caused by drinking instead returned a verdict of suicide during temporary insanity.

Emily Reynolds

With her eyes badly bruised, Emily, an elderly woman, who owned

Sychpant Farm, Abercarn, appeared at Blackwood police court in August 1904. She alleged her husband, William had given her the black eyes. There was a noticeable difference in the age of both. William appeared to be quite a young man compared to Emily.

Mr T. S. Edwards, advocate in the case suggested William fell in love with the farm and its stock more than with his wife. On the day of the assault, Mr Edwards stated that one of Emily's sons had visited the farm much to the annoyance of William. He was so annoyed that he hit Emily in a violent manner. Emily described the assault and said that William had knocked her down into a boiler and afterwards pulled her hair and beat her. William then said to Emily.

'Didn't you call me a lazy beggar?'

to which she replied

'Yes I have called you that many times'.

Dr. Smith of Abercarn said Emily had sustained severe bruising and he had found it necessary to place a stitch in one of the wounds over the eye.

Police Constable Lock said he had found Emily in an exhausted condition and bleeding from her head.

William alleged that Emily had irritated him by hitting him on the head with a big stone, though no evidence of this appears to have been presented.

The Bench concluded that William might have killed Emily but having regard to the provocation he received he was fined only five pounds with the alternative option of a month in prison.

Ann Davies

Ann, a widow, was summoned to Cwmbran police court in November 1906 by Llantarnam Urban District Council, to show cause why an order should not be made by the Bench for the closing of an alleged polluted well on her premises at Ty Coch. Mr H Haden, clerk to the council prosecuted and Mr G Thompson, county analyst said the well was nothing more than a cesspool for household filth. The water was so foul from animal waste that it was unfit to wash floors with. The Bench made a permanent closing order.

Cwmbran Polly

Elizabeth Crimmins was thirty seven years old in 1907. She appeared before Newport magistrates giving evidence against her husband, Michael who had been summoned for assault. She said that on Sunday morning, about 4 a.m. her husband got up and threatened to burn her, Her son came upstairs and took a lamp from him. Her husband then dragged her by the hair and thew her downstairs, about fourteen steps. He had been out of work for twelve months and she was keeping him.

Mr Digby Powell appeared for Michael and suggested he could not work due to his rheumatism. Elizabeth denied this and also denied the argument was caused by him wanting to go and live with his mother.

Henry Dunk, Elizabeth's son said that Michael had come home drunk. He went to bed and after about twenty minutes he heard his mother call him to come and take away the lamp as Michael was going to burn the bed. On going upstairs he found Michael holding his mother by the throat. He took the lamp away and returned to the kitchen. A short while after he heard Michael shout 'Go down there'. At the same time his mother rolled down the stairs and said 'Mike has done this'. She went upstairs again to get some clothing and he attacked her for a second time. Henry, who was following behind then hit Michael with an iron ornament, cutting his head. Michael was placed on the bed and Elizabeth attended to his wound. As he lay there he said 'Kiss me Lil, I am dying'. Then as she bent down to do so, he caught hold of her throat and almost strangled her.

Witness Mary Ann Kimbry, told the court she had been taken to the Crimmins' house by her 'sweetheart', Henry, for a nights lodging. They had been sitting in the kitchen when Mrs Crimmins called them upstairs, saying her husband was killing her. On going up they found the husband bleeding and being attended to by Elizabeth. She said she heard Mrs Crimmins fall downstairs but wasn't sure how it was done.

Mr Powell cross examined Mary Ann with regards to her character. It transpired she was well known in Newport but was from Cwmbran.

Mr Powell: 'And you are known as Cwmbran Polly?'

'Not to my face' she replied 'I am Mary Ann Kimbry. I think you are exceeding your rights there. I am not here to be insulted by you'.

Alderman Howell: 'Call her by her proper name Mr Powell'.

Leaving the box Mary Ann said to Mr Powell – 'I don't think much of your gentlemanliness, to try and drag a woman's name through the mire'.

Michael Crimmins stated the whole affair was an accident but the Bench sent him to prison for three months.

Mrs Sadler

Cwmbran witnessed a severe thunderstorm in July 1907 during which a thunderbolt fell and split a chimney stack in Pritchards Terrace. Mrs Sadler, an invalid, who was in bed at the time was rendered unconscious. Doctor Murphy was called and attended to her while other occupants of the house were alarmed but escaped any injury.

Margaret Ann Richards

Margaret's husband, Charles from Newbridge, was brought up in custody on remand at Abercarn charged with assaulting Margaret in June 1907. He was accused of beating her on the head with a poker, he pleaded guilty.

Dr. Thomas of Newbridge said on June 22nd he attended to Mrs Richards who had received a scalp wound abut five inches long and that her life had been in danger. Margaret stated her husband came home and asked for his supper. Phoebe Ann Turtle, servant said she then saw Mr Richards hit Margaret several times.

Police Constable Baker gave evidence of arrest and said Mr Richards told him he was annoyed as his supper was not ready. He was sentenced to six months hard labour.

Clara Greenway

Clara, of Cwmbran, summoned her husband, Albert Greenway, an iron moulder, aged 17, to court in July 1908. There she applied for a separation order on the grounds of desertion. They had been married in September 1907 and she stated that he was 'thoroughly lazy' For the previous five months they had been living off her mother but on May 16th he left and went to live with his mother in Gloucester. The Bench granted the separation and ordered him to pay four shillings weekly to his wife's maintenance.

Sarah Ann Neale

In May 1909, Sarah of Langstone, gave a list of excuses to Newport Magistrates when summoned for not sending her child to school.

'How am I able to send him to school. My husband went to Abergavenny nine years ago and I don't know whether he is alive or dead. I don't get parish relief, my boy is ill and the school is two and a half miles away. I will do my best after the holidays'.

The case was adjourned for inquiries.

Frances Williams

Frances was in court in November 1909 when her husband John was charged with cruelty to his children who were all under sixteen. Mr Lyndon Cooper prosecuted on behalf of the National Society for the Prevention of Cruelty to Children and described him as being shortsighted when looking for work. The family had been found in Langstone on 26th October in a very wet state Frances said she was married to John at Hereford registry office in April but went back to her mother as he cut her head and refused to work. She then went in to Westbury workhouse but he came and took her away on 24th October. They then went 'on the tramp'. On the day they left the workhouse they tramped for seven or eight miles and slept at a friends house. The following day which was very cold with showers they tramped twelve miles and that night took shelter under some trees. Next morning they headed off for Chepstow and that night Frances and her eldest daughter stayed in front of the fire at a lodging house. John and the two youngest daughters slept in a stable. This was not the first time he had tramped them around the country and had often refused work. John was committed to a trial at the next quarter sessions.

CRIME

Mary Ann Hanbury

Along with Catherine Andrews, Mary was committed to the House of Correction, for being a vagrant in the parish of Panteague in June 1842. They were sentenced to fourteen days each, with orders to be kept at hard labour.

Mary Jones

Mary was also sent to the House of Correction in June 1842. Her crime was that she was riotous at Pontypool workhouse and had assaulted another pauper. She was sentenced to fourteen days with hard labour.

Ann Jones

Newspapers often paid attention to how a woman looked or what she was wearing as if that had some bearing on the crime committed and the older the woman got the more derogatory the remarks, something that didn't happen quite as much with men. Ann was described in the Monmouthshire Merlin of 1849 as a 'wretched looking, shrivelled up old woman'. She was seventy nine years old and was charged with stealing a pound and a half of beef from Pontypool Market, the property of Abraham Jones. Witness, Ann

Morgan, proved that she saw Ann take the meat off the stall and walk away with it. Ann Morgan followed her, took the beef off her and returned it to the stall. Ann Jones then said that Ann Morgan had beaten her with a bone, so severely that she had not recovered from the effects. Ann Jones was found guilty and sent to the House of Correction for four weeks with appropriate labour.

Ann Hill

In May 1850, Ann went to the house of a poor woman who lived near Pontnewynydd. There she demanded alms but was refused. Ann then abused the woman and struck her with a poker. Neighbour, Mrs Bevan went to assist but Ann went and attacked her also and beat her. Ann was taken before the magistrates next morning where she was sent to prison for twenty one days.

Maria Davis

Maria of Cwmbran, brought up John Jones, a constable, in March 1854, on a charge of assaulting her with intent to commit a rape. A Mr Owen appeared for the constable and cross examined Maria and other witnesses at great length. Jones was sentenced to six weeks hard labour.

Eliza Price

Eliza was a coke worker who was charged with obtaining eight quarts of beer from Ann Jones, landlady of the Bridge Inn, Varteg Forge in September 1855. She had previously been in prison for three months for obtaining goods by false pretences. Mrs Jones stated that Eliza went to her house and said that Mr George Morgan and Mr Baker, gaffers at Golynos had sent her for three quarts of beer. This was given to her, then in the evening she came and obtained two more quarts. She brought no note but as Mrs Jones knew the gaffers she assumed the request was legitimate. Eliza carried on obtaining quarts of beer until her game was discovered and she appeared before the police court.

Ann Loomey

Also in September 1855, Ann was charged with stealing fifteen pounds of chalk, property of Abraham Darby, and others at the Abersychan works. P.C. Griffiths said he apprehended her with the lump of chalk in her possession. She said she found it among the ashes near the furnaces. James Ashman, a fitter at the British works stated that the chalk was the property of the prosecutors and had been in his care previously to it being taken from Ann. She acknowledged the theft and was tried at once. She pleaded guilty to the charge and was sentenced to one month's hard labour. Ann cried bitterly and became hysterical, the judge said he hoped the punishment would benefit her.

Emma Maggs

Emma, along with Jane Stone and Elizabeth Davies were charged in November 1855 with breach of the peace for burning an effigy and continually interrupting three women at Pontnewynydd. The demonstration was in consequence of the women having given evidence against a man before a magistrate. Elizabeth was proved to have said 'we are burning Mrs Splendid's image'. The man referred to was not even related to them so the Bench expressed disgust at the way the three demeaned themselves. They were bound over to keep the peace.

Elizabeth Harris

Elizabeth and her son Alfred were charged with committing a trespass on the property of Edward Blewitt at Llantarnam in April 1856. Mr Cathcart appeared in support of the charge and examined the pair at great length. They were the wife and son of James Harris, a tenant of Mr Blewitt who rented a corn mill and a few acres of land. They had had notice though to leave and both had been seen, at different times breaking down and carrying away the hedge. Elizabeth was discharged but Alfred had to pay two pounds nine shillings and six pence.

Sarah Prichard

Sarah was charged by Samuel Crew in April 1857 with assaulting him at Llantarnam. She was fined ten shillings and six pence costs.

Elizabeth Jones

In 1860 in Talywain, Elizabeth was charged with assaulting Elizabeth Powell. The argument had arisen because Elizabeth Powell had thrown some ashes on a footpath. Elizabeth Jones was fined one shilling plus twelve shillings expenses.

Catherine Talbot

Catherine, of the Rock, near Blackwood was described by the Monmouthshire Merlin as a 'miserable looking woman'. In August 1863 she was charged with committing wilful damage to some gooseberry trees, the property of Thomas Jones. She was fined six pence plus costs and in default, fourteen days in prison.

Amy Daniel

Amy lived with her uncle, on a farm in Nash, Newport. On a September evening in 1863, about half past five, she decided to go and visit a friend, alone. When going past the Newell farm, she spotted a man following her. His name was John Williams. As she reached the end of the farm fields that she had to walk through, she heard footsteps so she turned and saw John behind her. She decided to walk slower to let hm pass so he could go over a plank serving as a small bridge. He said 'Good evening Miss, are you going for a walk?' She answered that she was going as far as Salt Marsh. He asked if he could accompany her. She said that she was fine to go by herself. Then he said 'I must have a kiss'. 'No you wont' she answered. He then caught her round the waist and threw her to the ground. She screamed as he knelt on her and dragged up her clothes. She struggled, pulled his hair and tore his shirt. He in return scratched her face and hands. He was muttering to himself but she could not tell what. The struggle went on and he hurt her further. Thinking he might be trying to rob her she begged him to let her go and she would give him all her money. He asked her how much she had. She replied she didn't know but if he would let her up she would give him all she had. He let her up and she gave him all her money, six and a half pence. She then wasted no time, and ran off into a ditch, waded through water and hid under some briars in order to get away from him. Once he had left, she returned to retrieve her hat, umbrella and some apples but he came after her again. She jumped back into the ditch and up to her waist in water. He issued threats if she didn't come back out of the water but she waited until he got fed up and left. She then ran as fast as she could to a little cottage where the occupants helped her, gave her dry clothes and escorted her back to her uncle. A police constable went in pursuit of John who was apprehended at Chepstow. He asked the constable, 'What will be done to me?' The constable replied that he didn't know. John asked again, 'I wonder what they will do to me, I suppose they wont transport a fellow'. He also said that he was not guilty but was sent for trial anyway.

Emma Hughes

Emma, of Rhymney was charged in October 1864, with assaulting Ann Owens of the same place. It happened that they both lived near each other at Taibach, Rhymney and that their children quarrelled. They decided to follow suit. The Bench dismissed the case but divided the costs.

Ellen Rosser

Ellen and her husband John, a charcoal finer, both from Govilon were charged in October 1864 with stealing a quantity of drapery goods, property of the London and North Western Railway Company on 29 September. Ellen pleaded guilty and in a statement exonerated her husband from any share in the robbery and having also pleaded to two former convictions, she was sentenced to seven years penal servitude. Her husband was acquitted.

Maria Cole

For stealing various items of clothing, the property of Jeremiah Williams, in March 1867, Maria, a lodger with the Williams's, found herself in court. The value of the items came to three pounds. Mary Williams, daughter of Jeremiah, stated that she saw the items of clothing in the house before she went to work. On her return about five o clock both Maria and the clothes were gone.

Margaret Hanbury

At Newport petty sessions in July 1867 Margaret was charged with stealing a watch, the property of John Jones. There was no evidence offered against the accused except that she had lived for a short time as a servant and on the day named was left alone in the house. Mrs Jones said she saw the watch safe before she went out. As the day went on it was discovered that Margaret had left the house and it was found the watch was also missing. The police were called but they failed to locate Margaret for a short time until she was apprehended in Cardiff. In the meantime, Mrs Jones had a recurring dream that her husband's watch was in the hedge. She told neighbours of the dream and they urged her to take a look. Mrs Jones told them she did not believe in dreams and laughed at them. The neighbours did not give up though and eventually got Mrs Jones to look, and there it was! Margaret was discharged.

Elizabeth Powell

Elizabeth pleaded guilty in September 1868 to selling nine gallons of ale. The crime was not in the selling of the ale, she did so because she needed money to pay her rent. She was charged because she had no license. The bench fined her one shilling plus costs and in default of not being able to pay, one months imprisonment. Elizabeth went to prison, because she had nothing in the way of goods or cash to pay.

Martha Williams

Again the Monmouthshire Merlin pays great attention to the dress of the accused. Martha was described as a 'damsel, who sported a new black cloth jacket with velvet turn down collars, a la the other sex'. It devotes one line to her crime, she was charged with assaulting Emily Jones in Pontypool in 1870 and pleaded guilty though there was much provocation. It then continues with appearance, 'not withstanding the stylish get up of the defendant, the language on both sides was abominable and showed that fine feathers are not always to be depended upon as a test of the lady'. Martha was ordered to pay eleven shillings.

Mary Jane Munday

At the Sow hill, Pontypool in May 1870, Elizabeth Scrimmens, married, Margaret Scrimmens, Denis Scrimmens and their children, all Irish, were charged with assaulting Mary. The feud had occurred over the merits of Welsh or Irish, Roman Catholic or Methodist and arose through the children learning religious pieces to recite at a chapel anniversary. The language used by all was unfit for publication. The defendants were fined seven shillings and six pence each or seven days with hard labour.

Mary Harrington

Along with another woman, Mary Daley, Mary was charged with stealing coal, the property of John Lawrence of Cwmbran in January 1871. Both were described as respectable looking women, one with a baby in her arms. They pleaded guilty as P.C. Burley said he witnessed them taking the coal. They were given fourteen days hard labour.

Elizabeth Ashcroft

Henry Jones subjected Elizabeth to an unprovoked attack in January 1871. Neither knew each other, but on passing Henry and his companions in Trosnant, Elizabeth was rudely stared at. The incident must have frightened her as she remarked to a man and woman who were with her that Henry would 'know her' next time. Henry then said 'Yes you b.....,, I'll make you know me'. He approached her and proceeded to hit her several times in the face as well as her woman friend. He was fined two pounds plus costs.

Mary Hannan

Cornelius Hannan, a middle aged Irishman was charged with killing and slaying his wife Mary at Abersychan. She died from injuries inflicted on 17th March 1871, St Patrick's Day. Cornelius was remanded so an inquest could be held and was charged with manslaughter.

It was revealed in the police court that Mary received a blow to the head and died on 24th March. She was Cornelius's second wife and left a son who was four and a half years old.

The Hannan's lodged at the house of James and Ellen Lane. On March 17th James and Cornelius came home and had supper after which Cornelius and Mary had words about what drapery should be paid for out of the next pay. Cornelius said his boy should have some clothes while Mary said she would like a new petticoat and frock. They then argued and Cornelius got up, pulled Mary by the hair and hit her on the head with a clenched fist.

After the attack Mary sat on a bench by the fire while Cornelius went out. An old woman named Mrs Hide then came to the house and began singing a song. Mary joined in but while doing so fell with her head in Mrs Hide's lap where she was sick. Mary appeared drunk but had only had a share of three pints of beer between seven people. Mary's body became stiff and she was carried to bed by Mrs Hide and Mr and Mrs Lane.

Next morning Mrs Hide went to check on Mary, then sent for the doctor. At this point, Mary could speak but no one could understand what she was saying. She got worse until she died on 24th March.

Dr. John Davies stated he found Mary with a severe injury to her brain. When he visited Mary recognised him to begin with but then became insensible. A post mortem revealed bleeding in her brain resulting from ruptured blood vessels

Ann Vaughn

Ann went to buy a pennyworth of hair oil from a widow in Woodland Row, Pontypool in February 1872. The widow lived with a man, Michael Kelly. She was glad to see Ann and not long after some other women arrived. They all began drinking beer and brandy and were enjoying themselves until Kelly came in and started calling Ann names. Then he hit her. When cross examined in court Ann admitted to drinking and had taken the brandy and beer to the house herself, hidden under her clothes. She denied being out all night and wanting a little girl who was present to go and pawn some items for her. Mary Mahoney, the widow said she was Kelly's housekeeper, that Ann was very drunk and Kelly only shoved her out because she would not leave. The case was dismissed.

Leah Powell

At Pontypool police court in June 1872, Leah was charged with assaulting Mary Jane Williams at Garndiffaith. It seemed that during a thunderstorm Leah wanted to fill her bucket with some water from a spout near Mary Jane's house. Mary objected and a row developed resulting in the throwing of water over each other. Leah was fined fourteen shillings.

Mary Watkins

Also in June 1872, Mary was charged with using violent threats towards Jane Edwards of Pontnewynydd and assaulting Jane's daughter Mary Ann. Some very filthy language was used and neighbours stated Jane was a disgrace to the place and it was she and her daughter who were the aggressors. The case was dismissed and the Edwards' paid the costs.

Blanche Edwards

At the Newport petty sessions in July 1873, Blanche was charged with assaulting Jane Coles. Jane said she was a char woman to Blanche, who kept a disreputable house in Lewis Street. Anna McGuire, gave evidence in favour of Blanche and said that Jane had struck Blanche and then had thrown herself on the sofa like a beast. It appeared Jane had been sent out to buy meat and on return was drunk. She had also brought meat that was too fat. A dispute arose and Anna stated how thousands of people gathered in the street and she, Anna, called a police officer. P C Dovey said that a large crowd had assembled outside the house and Jane was inside tumbling about in an intoxicated manner. Anna said there were three young ladies in the house, and she was one of them. The case was dismissed.

Elizabeth Jones

On the same date as the above account, Elizabeth, a brothel keeper of 1 Dolphin Street was charged on a warrant with assaulting Ann Wood. Ann said she came from Abergavenny and lived for eight months with Elizabeth and at the end of that time had left, due to being insufficiently clothed and fed. Elizabeth had since been in the habit of abusing and molesting her when they met in the street. On a Friday night, they met in Dolphin Street and Elizabeth kicked her down and continued to kick her. Ann could not defend herself due to the number of other men and women Elizabeth had with her.

In answer to a question from the Bench, it was stated by the Superintendent of police that Elizabeth's house was the subject of many complaints. Witness Jane Smith said she saw Elizabeth knock Ann down and kick her across the road. Elizabeth did not deny the assault but called a witness to show that Ann was the aggressor.

The magistrates considered a violent assault had taken place and that Elizabeth's house was a nuisance to the neighbourhood. They decided to sentence Elizabeth to one month's hard labour and proceeded to take steps to shut the house down.

Hannah Lewis

It was December 1877 that Hannah, wife of William who lived at Alma Cottage in Bedwas was charged with stealing four pounds and ten shillings in gold that belonged to Thomas Cobby, a collier who lodged with her. Thomas, asked the Bench to dismiss the charge as Hannah was the mother of five small children. The charge was dismissed..

Alice Ann Holder

A fowl was annoying Alice in 1879, the property of Anne Williams. Alice stole the fowl and took it to Thomas Lewis, a butcher in Pontypool. She was charged with the offence and her plea was that it was a nuisance to her and she could not keep it out of her house. She was sentenced to a day in prison.

Annie Cordey

Before Colonel Byrde, at Pontypool police court in January 1879, Annie was charged with taking water belonging to the Pontypool Water Company without paying for it. She pleaded not guilty.

P.C. Saunders stated that at five in the afternoon on the 23rd December, he saw a little girl, Ellen Evans come out of Annie's house with a tin. She went into her mother's house and filled the tin with water from the tap. When she came out he asked her for whom she was fetching the water, and Ellen replied 'for Mrs C'. He then told her she must not fetch anymore water for Annie.

Annie pleaded that she gave the little girl a penny a day for fetching water from Lasgarn Wood and she did not know that Ellen had not gone there for it. She could not drink water from a tap as it did not agree with her. Ellen Evans corroborated the story and the charge was dismissed.

Charlotte Moore

Charlotte was charged with vagrancy in February 1882, by wandering around and having no visible means of subsistence at Trosnant, Pontypool. Constable Williams stated he saw her coming up Trosnant followed by a crowd of children. She appeared to be out of her senses and conducted herself in a very strange manner. It was stated that numerous complaints had been made to the police. Charlotte went in to people's houses and they would then have great difficulty in getting her back out. Charlotte exclaimed that people were mad and she was the one who was right. She described how the children pelted her with stones and dirt. The Chairman stated that she was in such a bad condition that care needed to be taken of her and so they sent her to Usk prison for seven days.

Emily Kenny

Emily was charged in 1884 with stealing a dress and various items of clothing. She was employed by Mr Henry Studd, a well known showman. It was her job to look after a shooting gallery. On Bank Holiday, Mr Studd had his whole establishment at a fete in Tredegar Park and Mrs Studd lent Emily some clothing for the day, telling her to place the articles in one of the vans at the end of the day. Instead, Emily returned to her normal clothes, folded the others into a bundle and went to her mother's house in Newport. She was later apprehended and charged with stealing. It was discovered on cross examination that her wages were fourteen shillings a month but she had not received any money for the last quarter. Mrs Studd had spent Emily's wages on her clothes. The magistrates thought, under the circumstances, Emily may have believed she had a right to the clothing and suggested that the matter should be dropped. Emily was discharged.

Sarah Redman

On 5th November, 1885, Sarah, a married woman was summoned for throwing fireworks in the street in Usk. Two policemen said she committed the act in defiance of them. She was fined five shillings and ten pence costs.

Catherine Ford

Catherine was charged with being drunk and disorderly in Ebbw Vale on 9th October 1886. When asked what she had to say about the charge she stated that her brother was in the habit of coming to her house and beating her. He also smashed her windows. On the day in question he called and hit her head so violently against a wall that she was rendered drunk with the blow. She was not drunk with beer but from the impact of her head against the wall. The Bench however didn't believe her and fined her five shillings.

Mary Ann Waldron

At Newport County police court in April 1888, Frederick Howells, aged fifteen was charged with stealing hay, property of Lord Tredegar, and Mary, who was said to be dressed in 'weeds' was charged with receiving the hay, knowing it was stolen.

Edward Little, a hay cutter from Christchurch said he had cut one hundred and nine trusses of hay at Cwm Farm, Christchurch and later found he was missing one. P.S. Pask went to Mary's house and asked for Frederick who was in her employ. Mary denied any knowledge of the hay but Frederick said she had helped him convert the hay into chaff. Mary had a pony and made a living for herself and her four children by selling milk. She was almost blind and Frederick was virtually an orphan. The Bench sentenced both to one day in prison.

Elizabeth Owen

At Abercarn petty sessions in November 1897, Elizabeth charged her sister in law Ellen James with assault on November 1st in Wattsville, North Risca. There was also a summons by Mrs James against Jonathan Owen, Elizabeth's son. Someone had kicked Mrs James's door and she confronted Jonathan about it. It was then hostilities commenced. Ellen was fined ten shillings plus costs while the charge against Jonathan was dismissed on payment of costs.

Elizabeth Davies

Michael Mountain, a well known character in Brynmawr appeared at police court charged with grievous bodily harm against Elizabeth. It was alleged Michael's sister went to Elizabeth's house and asked her to give a reason for a statement that

'She did not know how she and her brother (Michael) got their living'.

Michael, who was waiting nearby then assaulted Elizabeth, fracturing her lower jaw. He was set to assizes for trial.

Frances Mary Powell

Frances, a schoolmistress, of the Post Office, Llanfrechfa charged Walter Pritchard in August 1898 with aggravated assault. The court was crowded as Mr Horace Lyne prosecuted on behalf of the police and said that in the district the general feeling was to hush the whole case up and he was not sure why. The peculiarities of the case was a youth of fifteen assaulting a young woman with no motive for the crime and added that if Frances and her friends had had their way no proceedings would have taken place at all.

Frances had left her house with a lady friend at around nine in the evening to go to Pontypool. Passing Church Road they saw a group of men, one of whom, George White spoke to her. It was unclear whether Walter was there.

Frances parted company with her friend and on her way back home, she passed a gate. At this gate someone sprang out of the opening. He grabbed her neck and pulled her head about. She thought it was Walter and said 'Oh Walter, don't'.

Frances lost consciousness but when she came round she was near a hedge opposite the gate. Her head was bleeding on one side. She remembered Walter being brought to her house afterwards and him saying 'I didn't do it'. She was asked to sign a statement to say she was happy Walter had not attacked her, though she was advised not to. She had always been friendly with Walter and was unaware of any reason for him to assault her.

A doctor from Caerleon then spoke of finding Frances at home on the kitchen floor, her head bandaged. Her hair and clothing was saturated with blood and there were two wounds just above her ear. The upper wound extended to the bone of the skull. She also had bruises on her left arm which was thought to have been caused by a heavy object such as the piece of iron that was produced.

For the defence, Mr Llewellyn stated a young man, quiet and inoffensive could not have dealt blows to her with such a weapon. There was nothing in Walter's conduct to find him guilty however the court did and Walter was fined five pounds and three pounds and five shillings costs.

Alice Taylor

At the Abercarn petty sessions in April 1899, Dick Crowther, thirty two, from Newbridge was charged with attempting to outrage Alice, aged thirty and a married woman who lived at Celynen Terrace, Newbridge. It was alleged by the prosecution that the defendant, while drunk, entered Alice's house while her husband was away, locked the door behind him and was violent towards her, all the while ignoring her screams. Ultimately he fell over a chair and she managed to escape to a neighbour's. He said he visited her home with her consent. The case was dismissed.

Margaret Franklin

Margaret's was the first case that came before Newport magistrates, to be tried under the Habitual Inebriates Act. She had been drunk in Shaftesbury Street in January 1900 and it was her fourth appearance in twelve months. She was set to the Victoria Home in Bristol for three years.

Johannah Hennessy

Johannah, a married woman of no abode was sent to prison for seven days in February 1901 for sleeping rough in an outhouse at Riverside, Merthyr. She was found asleep with a man but, as he had money in his pocket, he was discharged.

Annie Driscoll

Before the Cwmbran magistrates in May 1905, Annie of Raglan Terrace appeared with her sister in law, Mary Ann Leyshon, an elderly woman. Both had taken summonses out as both were on bad terms with each other and had been for some time. On the 15th May, Annie had thrown a bucket of water over Mary. This annoyed Mary so much she smashed the window panes in Annie's house with her fist. Annie then threw a jug of water over her too.

Mr Pilliner said to Annie – 'If you are not careful you will be summoned for wasting water'.

The Bench bound them over and ordered Mary to pay damages of one shilling.

Ellen Morgan

At Cwmbran police court in December 1906, Ellen, a tramp, was charged with stealing a silver brooch, a skirt and a pair of boots, the property of Owen Phillips of Penypark Farm, Llantarnam. She was seen loitering about the place and was assumed to have entered by the front door, unobserved and then walked upstairs and stole the articles from one of the bedrooms. She was arrested in Newport later in the evening by Sergeant Morris to whom she admitted her guilt. She was sent to prison with one month hard labour.

Mrs Jenkins

Mrs Jenkins of Maesteg was a suffragette and in the Cardiff Times of 6 April 1907, spoke about her imprisonment for demonstrating in London. She said she had been far from well during her incarceration and had had a violent cold. She was not well when arrested.

'I came to London' she went on 'with the full sanction of my husband and fully determined to go to prison. Though I have been unwell and have nearly lost my voice, I would not go to hospital. I, however, saw the doctor and had a vegetarian diet which included three pints of milk a day and vegetables. I am very glad I did come to London and have gone to gaol for the cause and you can tell the women of Wales so. There are a good many women in Maesteg who would like to come but they cannot get away'.

Another suffragette, Miss Arscott of Merthyr said that she had found things very decent after her first day in Holloway.

'After then' she said 'I asked to be put on a vegetarian diet and got three pints of milk a day. But the first day – Ugh! They sent me some horrible tinned stuff, one taste of which was enough. I tried one mouthful, I could touch no more but when I had seen the doctor and asked for a vegetarian diet it was better, though I am not a vegetarian. The solitary confinement was dreadfully irksome. I am not sorry I came to London – far from it. In fact, I shall come again and a good any more shall come with me next time'.

These Welsh Suffragettes returned home after their two weeks of imprisonment. Referring to their demonstration at Westminster on March 20th for which they were brought up at the police court on the charge of disorderly conduct and resisting the police, they denied that they were disorderly and said it was the men and the boys in the crowd who were the offenders.

Another Suffragette, Miss Phillips observed -

'They made more fuss than we did, a lot'.

All seemed genuinely disappointed their demonstration was not more successful – it was their first offence at Westminster but they could not say if it would be their last.

Grace Isles

In the Newport Union workhouse in April 1908, Grace was charged with assaulting and beating Janet Goulding and Bessie Davies, a nurse. Superintendent Brookes said Grace was too ill to go to the dock from the cells as she had been ill all night.

Alderman Mordey asked if she could be remanded for a few days and if so could she stay in the cells. The Sergeant said it would be alright to do so, unless she could be taken to the workhouse. The Alderman expressed his concern at Grace being kept in the cells under the circumstances. A doctor was called and after an examination he said Grace could not attend court. Grace was remanded to the workhouse infirmary instead.

Cecilia Harris

Cecilia was a widow who lived alone in a secluded farm on

Lasgarn mountain, near Abersychan. On a Saturday night in February 1909 she saw a man loitering near the farm, he was carrying a gun. Cecilia knew who the man was and told him to go away but instead he aimed the gun at her though it misfired. Cecilia rushed back into her house, locked the doors and went to her bedroom. She then heard the sound of falling glass. The man entered the house through a window and again fired at her. This time he didn't miss and the charge lodged in her mouth and right side of her face. He then picked up a table knife and cut her throat, inflicting a terrible wound. Cecilia, somehow summoned strength to crawl out of the house and was able to reach a neighbour at Penyrheol Farm, half a mile away!

At the neighbour's farm, a doctor and the police were sent for, Dr. McCormac of Abersychan, Superintendent James and P.S. Jones. Cecilia was too weak to speak but managed to write down the name of her attacker, she was then taken to Pontypool Hospital.

John Edmunds, a collier, was arrested in the High Street, Garndiffaith and taken to the police station. He was later taken to the hospital where he was identified by Cecilia as her attacker. John pleaded his innocence and said 'I know nothing about it'. The police sergeant locked him up.

A reporter from the South Wales Daily News examined the farm and reported on it for the paper, it was

'approached by a long narrow lane and in the centre of several large meadows.'

The house appeared to have been built in the 1700s. The window sill was stained with blood and the reporter could trace the movement of Cecilia between her farm and Penyrheol as every stile and gate was spattered with blood.

Cecilia died at Pontypool Hospital in May 1909. She made enough of a recovery to be able to attend police court where, as a result of her evidence, John was committed to the assizes for trial. There, he was sentenced to death. He appealed the decision in June 1909, but it was refused. John was hanged in Monmouth County Gaol for the murder of Cecilia Harris the following month. Before his execution he had a comfortable room, smoked many cigarettes and read some books. He showed no remorse at all but maintained he was innocent.

Ellen Allen

On September 5th 1910, Ellen of St Dials Road, Cwmbran was summoned for assaulting Ishmael Jones, her next door neighbour. Hannah, Ishmaels's wife was also summoned for making threats to Ellen and both were summoned for assaulting Ellen.

The Jones's stated that Ellen had been parading up and down outside their house for about two hours, inviting them to go out and fight. At about ten o clock Hannah had occasion to go outside and Ellen then struck her a violent blow across her head with a tray. Ishmael went outside and saw Ellen assault Hannah and just as he was helping her get back in the house, Ellen came up with a knife and struck at him saying, 'Take that you ----, I will have blood for supper tonight'. Ishmael felt a sharp stinging pain in his face and sustained a severe cut three and a half inches long from which he lost a significant amount of blood. He was unable to work for about three weeks in consequence.

David Jones, son of Ishmael, stated that on returning home on the morning of September 6th he picked up a blood stained table knife at the spot where his father had been assaulted. Ellen stated that Hannah had brought serious allegations against her and struck her across the face with a tray, blackening her eye and that Ishmael had held her while letting his wife continue to beat her. She said she did not use a knife at any time. After a private deliberation the Bench fined Ellen three pounds or one month in prison in default. Hannah was fined a pound and the summons against Ishmael was dismissed.

WORK

Molly Hanbury Leigh

Molly was already a wealthy widow when she married Capel Hanbury Leigh in September 1797. She was a collector of shells and it is believed she designed the interior of the shell grotto in Pontypool Park.   She was also involved in charity work and did much to relieve the suffering of the poor in Pontypool.

A Strike

No names to mention in this snippet of news from the Monmouthshire Merlin of 13 July 1850. The female hay-makers at the farm of the British Iron Company, went on strike for an increase in their wages.

Elizabeth Jones

An accident occurred in one of the mine patches in Blaenavon in March 1860 resulting in the death of Elizabeth who was just 16 years old. A heavy mass of earth fell, in which she was embedded, together with a man who was working at the same spot. When they were extricated from the debris it was found that the man's legs and other parts of his body were badly bruised but Elizabeth was dead. Her body was mutilated, her head being so badly crushed that her brain protruded and she had to be buried with her clothes on. Another little girl who was picking mine, close to the spot very narrowly escaped.

Emily Woffadon

Emily was 16 in April 1860 and was employed by Mr Clayfield, a shoemaker of George Street, Pontypool. While in work, she placed her boot on the top bar of the fireplace for the purpose of lacing up her boot, when her dress came into contact with fire. She was seriously burned and lay in a precarious state though it is not known whether she survived or not.

Sarah Williams

The age to which women could be working until was recorded in an article in the Illustrated Usk Observer in February 1863. It concerned Sarah who was 78 yeas old. She was attending to domestic duties in a bakehouse in Blaenavon when she dropped down dead.

Elizabeth Heslop

Elizabeth was landlady of the Gardeners Arms in Llanarth. She was in court in February 1863 for having her house open for the sale of beer during prohibited hours on Christmas Day. She was cautioned and ordered to pay costs.

Miss Jones

At the Girls National School in March 1863, in Blaenavon, Miss Jones was presented with a rosewood writing desk by the pupils under her superintendence and a few friends, as a token of the high regard in she was held . It was her last week in her role as mistress at the school, it was likely she was leaving due to marriage.

Florence Williams

Lawrence Williams was charged with throwing a stone through the window of the Lower Cock Inn, Croesyceiliog in April 1866. He had been drinking in the house and for some offence had been turfed out by landlady, Florence. He was fined thirty shillings.

Sophia Williams

Sophia was the landlady of Joseph Parfitt and in January 1867 a few harsh words had been exchanged between the two. Joseph said Sophia had thrown a knife at him and hit him in the forehead. Sophia said Joseph had claimed he had paid five shillings and nine pence for lodgings when he had only paid three shillings and eight pence. She said he had also hit her children and given one a black eye. The case was dismissed.

Margaret Bevan

In July 1867, Margaret was indicted for unlawfully keeping a disorderly house in Trevethin. Police Constable Basham said Margaret kept the Parrot Beer House. He had been in the habit of calling at the house where Margaret was the landlady. One night he went to the house and found two prostitutes and two men in bed in one room and a prostitute and a man in another. One woman, Mary Ann James, said she gained her living by prostitution and had been to Margaret's house several times with men. Margaret's sentence was deferred.

Mrs Thomas

On Saturday 22nd August 1868 in Blaenavon, the Reverend R.P. Hill presented Mrs Thomas, governess of Blaenavon endowed schools, with a 'Queen Mab' sewing machine accompanied by a note in which he expressed the hope 'That it would prove as useful to her as she was to the Blaenavon school'.

Mrs Roberts

On the 13th April 1869, a fire broke out in the warehouses belonging to Mrs Roberts's china shop. She worked as a woollen, flannel and furniture dealer. The fire was discovered early in the morning but not before it had taken a strong hold on one of the warehouses. A great deal of stock was burned and some things saved were damaged in the process of rescuing them. The roof of one of the warehouses fell in. It was not discovered how the fire began.

Sarah Ann Nicholas

In the Monmouthshire Merlin of 12 February 1870, Sarah was described as a 'tip wench'. She was in court trying to recover money due to her from John Lewis of Blaenavon. The Merlin described her entrance into the witness box

'Complainant came into the witness box in the usual costume of the sisterhood, the 'tip wenches', a literal bundle of filthy rags. This was somewhat remarkable as these ladies generally came out on Sundays and state occasions in the extreme of fashion and excite wonder as to 'how do they do it'.

John was ordered to pay her three shillings and sixpence a week until the debt was cleared off and two shillings and sixpence a week afterwards. He requested time to pay the costs but as Superintendent Mackintosh thought that he would bolt, he was told he must pay at once or go to prison.

Elizabeth Jarratt

In November 1870, Elizabeth was charged with pretending to tell fortunes and obtaining money for it. It was a fact many people, including ones belonging to the 'respectable classes' had sought her advice for years. However, one day two servant girls, Ann Radford and Harriet Rogers went and gave her half a crown. She told their fortunes with the cards and told them a fortune that led them to go away to look for 'sweethearts'. Radford returned the following Monday and swallowed laudanum, as she said for the purpose of curing stomach ache but the dose was too large, though her life was saved. Elizabeth was sent to gaol for one month with hard labour.

In July, the following year, Elizabeth was in court again, making a complaint against a lady called Mrs Shufflebottom, who, to show her disapproval of fortune tellers had splattered Elizabeth's house with dirt and broke her windows. This led to her being charged with trespass and fined twelve shillings and sixpence.

Catherine Lewis

Catherine worked at a stall in Pontypool Market. In February 1872 she was in court accusing Margaret Frances of assault. Margaret said that Catherine had been scandalizing her character and when she went to ask why, she hit her with no provocation. Catherine said that Margaret came to her stall in a very drunk state and said she would not stop annoying her as long as she had a faggot to sell. Catherine was annoyed and jumped over the stall and she and Margaret had a 'set to'. They asked men nearby to see that there was fair play and which was the best woman. Police Sergeant Barham said Margaret was very drunk when she called into the police station to make a complaint. The case was dismissed.

Isabella Evans

Isabella was seventeen in September 1873 when she was injured in an accident at work. Her employer was Mr Williams of the Market Tavern, Abercarn and the injuries occurred when she accidentally fell into a tub of boiling beer while reaching for a strainer. She scalded the lower part of her body and Mr Williams, on hearing her screams rushed to her aid and got her out. Dr. Davies of Pentwynmawr was sent for and all was done to try and ease her suffering.

Ann Richards

A case of suicide was investigated by coroner, E D Batt and jury in May 1874. Ann, of Flannel Street, Abergavenny had committed suicide by throwing herself into the River Usk. Dr. Smythe said she had been a patient of his and had been suffering from depression of spirits. About three or four years earlier she had entered into a large business and appeared to be afraid that the undertaking would ruin her. He had no idea that she was thinking of killing herself until her nephew informed him that she had been seen by the river in suspicious circumstances. Dr. Smythe told the nephew that she would require looking after and suggested he should make arrangements to send her to friends for a change of scenery but if she did not go she would be required to go into an asylum. The despondency was attributed to delusions with regard to the business.

The jury returned a verdict in accordance with the medical evidence.

Lucy Thompson

Lucy was thirteen in August 1876. She was a servant employed by Frederick Williams, landlord of the Steam Packet Inn, Newport. He was charged with a violent assault upon her. Lucy said she had been tempted by another servant, Mary Niblett, to rob the till. She took two shillings and eight pence and put it in a box, where it was found. She then said that Mr Williams called her upstairs and said as a result of the theft he would fetch a policeman. Lucy said she picked the money up off the lodgers bed. Williams told her to go to her room. He then called her again and told her to go into a room at the back of the inn and undress. She did as she was told and took off all she had. When Williams entered the room she was naked. He got a rope with two or three knots, shut the door and put her on the bed. He put his knees on her back, beat her with the rope and told her to tell the truth. Mary, the other servant said that she didn't tell her to take any money, so Williams ordered Lucy back to her room where he beat her again. He also tied her hands with rope and hitched her onto the bedpost. Her feet didn't touch the ground but eventually she got her hands free and managed to run out into the street, still naked. A man named George Price saw her outside. Her wrists were red and her back was purple and covered in wheals. George took her to a policeman. P.C. Williams stated that blood was oozing from some of the wheals. Mr R. Cooke, surgeon, examined her right leg and part of her buttocks and found they were a mass of bruises. She seemed to have had a general thrashing. There was the appearance of a kick on her buttock. Her wrists were swollen but not bruised.

Mr Graham, acting on behalf of Frederick Williams, did not deny the child was beaten but denied she was tied to a bedpost. Mr Graham called the servant, Mary who said the beating was given in the sitting room and Lucy was not naked then. There was no bedstead in the room and she denied telling Lucy to take anything but Lucy repeated that she did. Frederick Williams was fined five pounds in costs.

Ann Pritchards

At the Caerleon petty sessions, Ann, the landlady of the

Wheatsheaf Inn, Llantarnam, was summoned for keeping her house open for the sale of drink during prohibited hours on Sunday 8th October 1889. P C Morgan watched her premises from a spot about forty yards away and saw a number of men drinking. On going closer to the house he was spotted by the men who quickly ran. One man who was caught gave a false name. Thirteen were counted outside of the house and five inside. Ann told the officer she could not help it and could not explain why either. It was ploughing match day and she had been very busy. Superintendent Bosanquet said the house was in a very out of the way place and afforded great facilities for carrying on an illicit trade. Ann was not present at court and the Bench took this absence as contempt of court. She was fined fifty shillings together with an endorsement on her license, in default, one month in prison.

Mary Jane Harvey

Mr Batt, coroner, held an inquest at the Rifleman's Arms, Blaenavon in June 1893 respecting the death of Mary. She was seventeen years old and had been a servant in the employ of Mr Cooke, draper. There had been some 'unpleasantness' at work and Mary left on 9th June. After that she seemed to have something on her mind. The last time she was seen alive was 11th June on the Abergavenny Road, about a mile from Blaenavon. All searches for her failed until finally her body was found in Balls pond by a milkman named James. Dr. Quirke stated that the body had the appearance of having been in the water for about a week. A verdict of found drowned was returned.

Mary Ann Davies

On 15th May 1897, Margaret Hunt visited Mary who was landlady of the Mill Tavern in Cwmbran. It was half past eleven in the morning and Margaret smashed every window in the house. She used a small revolver to smash some and threw other articles at the rest. She also visited on the 21st and said to Mary – 'I'll kill you and you'll never live to tell who did it'. Margaret also took charge of the bar and gave away whiskey and beer. She turned on the taps in the cellar and let the beer run to waste. Margaret pleaded guilty and told the court that Mary had been living with her husband (Mr Hunt was gardener at the Mill Tavern) Mr Hunt also stated his wife was a loose woman. The Bench decided Margaret had received great provocation and only ordered her to pay thirty shillings for the damage. Mary had to pay the costs.

Sarah Stokes

Sarah, who also went by the surname of Pearson, was a travelling gypsy who was brought before Abercarn magistrates in January 1901 on a charge of obtaining one pound and ten shillings by claiming to tell fortunes in North Risca on 15th December 1900. A young man named George Harris who was captivated with the old woman, told her he did not know where his father lived. Sarah said she could help him but he had to give her some silver, so he gave her a crown. Sarah went away, but returned requesting more money to complete her tracing. The next time she visited she said it was with good news however she needed some gold, just to be sure. The young man gave her more money but was receiving no information about his father in return.

Sarah was fined one pound and costs.

Hannah Hutchings

Hannah was the landlady of the Railway Inn in Cwmbran in September 1903. A collier, James Smith came into her inn on the above date and assaulted her. She said he came in and demanded a drink. She saw he was drunk and asked him to leave but he refused to go and then caught hold of her by the throat and bit her finger. He was fined six shillings or two months in prison.

Margaret Elias

In Victoria Street, Cwmbran, Margaret ran a baking business. In December 1903, a haulier, Thomas Edwin Evans aged 21 was charged with stealing a set of silver mounted pony harnesses from her. A large number of witnesses were called and the hearing lasted for several hours. The Bench committed him to a trial at the next quarter sessions. Bail was allowed in two sureties of ten pounds.

Frances Williams

Malpas Street, Cwmbran was the location of Frances's lodging house. David Jones, a brickmaker was charged in April 1905 with attempting to 'commit an offence upon her'. At Usk quarter sessions, Frances was greatly distressed and had to be given a chair. She related that Jones had rushed at her and tried to assault her. She screamed and so people came to her aid. Jones though, declared that she had attacked him with a poker because he was sitting in her late husband's chair. A struggle followed and they were rolling around on the floor when the neighbours came in. Jones was found guilty and sentenced to nine months hard labour.

Martha Smith

A simple task such as going on an errand could be fraught with danger, as Martha found out in November 1908. She was employed as a cook at the Rectory in Langstone, near Newport and was taking a letter to a nearby letterbox when she was attacked by a man who jumped off his bicycle. Her dog attacked the man but he kicked it into a fence. A postman's whistle was then heard. The man violently struck Martha on the side of her head and rode off. It was the third time such an attack had happened in the area.

SOCIAL LIFE

Clara Balfour

Clara delivered a lecture on Home Influence and Early Impressions in Ebbw Vale in September 1855. The spacious lecture room at the Scientific and literary Institution was filled with people, among the audience the leading gentry and tradesmen of the district. The Reverend Mr Morgan proposed a vote of thanks to Mrs Balfour and the audience left, very pleased with her talk.

Mrs Watkins

Mrs Watkins, the hostess of the Market Tavern, Abercarn, held another of her annual suppers in March 1856 which was attended by around forty people. Entertainment was provided by harpists and violinists. The guests dispersed at a late hour pleased with the excellent catering.

Miss Montague

Miss Montague, was renowned for her feats in connection with mesmerism. In January 1859 she gave a performance of 'animal magnetism' in the Town Hall in Pontypool. The Cardiff Times wrote that her demonstrations of occult science and mysteries of mesmerism were so great that crowds who had gathered hoping to witness her powers were unable to obtain admission

In February 1859, the residents of Blaenavon were witness to a performance of electro-biology by Miss Montague. It was very popular, her performance in the Temperance Hall in Merthyr was attended by more than a thousand people and hundreds more were unable to obtain admission.

Miss Montague worked most evenings and many people were operated on and made to perform antics for the amusement of the crowd. Her audiences were said to be kept in roars of laughter and always enjoyed her performances.

Lizzy Stuart

The Monmouthshire Merlin reported a 'pleasant entertainment' at the Literary and Scientific Institute, Ebbw Vale in February 1860, by Lizzy. She was an interpreter of Scottish songs that attracted a large audience and with songs such as 'Auld Robin Grey', 'The Flowers of the Forest', 'My Nannie's awa'' and 'Bonnie Prince Charlie', she was greatly admired.

Madame E L Williams

Also known as the 'Welsh Nightingale, Madame Williams gave a performance called 'Capers and Counterfeits' at the Town Hall, Blaenavon in January 1864. The hall was crowded and the Monmouthshire Merlin reported that everyone seemed to thoroughly enjoy it and appreciate the various characters and songs in which she appeared.

Female Benefit Society

The 'Odd Sisters' held their anniversary at the house of Mr John Vincent, the Prince of Wales Inn in Blaenavon in November 1864. Around two hundred attended both members and friends. Tea was served and credit given to Mrs Vincent and her staff. The club room was decorated for the occasion, then dancing rounded off the evening.

Miss Evans

Miss Evans delivered a lecture in August 1866 at the Welsh Calvinistic Methodist Chapel in Ebbw Vale. The subject was 'Children and their Education'. The lecture was for the benefit of the chapel though the audience was not as large as on other occasions when Miss Evans lectured. However it was an informative one and left a positive impression on the audience stated the Monmouthshire Merlin.

Miss J Rees

In Blackwood in September 1867, the Drill Hall was filled to hear a lecture by Miss Rees who was also known as 'Cranog – Wen'. The audience was riveted by her speech, the Monmouthshire Merlin recorded. The Chairman was the Reverend D Hughes and the lecture was for the benefit of the Calvinistic Methodist Chapel at Gelligroes.

Emma Stanley

Emma, considered a 'talented lady' by the South Wales Advertiser appeared at the Literary and Scientific Institution Hall, Ebbw Vale in March 1871. She gave an entertainment entitled 'Seven Ages of Woman'. The hall was filled to capacity long before the proceedings took place and in the audience were many influential families from the town and surrounding district. Miss Stanley was enthusiastically received and was a great favourite in the town.

Miss Deakin

A successful concert of vocal and instrumental music was held at the White Horse Assembly Rooms, Blaenavon in April 1871. Miss Deakin played the piano and Miss M A Witchell played the harmonium. The singing and music consisted of solos, duets, quartets and choruses, consisting of sacred music and temperance melodies. The proceeds were applied to the funds for opening a new day school in connection with the Wesleyan church.

Mrs Johns

The Ladies Committee held a meeting in Blackwood in September 1873 and Mrs Johns of Bedwelty Vicarage was Chairwoman. The meeting was in connection with a church bazaar. The honourable secretary Reverend T Theophilus entered into a statement of the accounts that the proceeds after expenses was sixty one pounds.

Mrs Edgcombe

A public entertainment was given in the Wesley Hall, Cwmbran in October 1879 consisting of glees, duets and solos by the Newport Bible Christian Choir assisted by Mrs Edgcombe and friends. The hall was crowded and all proceeds went to the chapel fund. Tea was also provided for the visitors.

Lady Barnard

She lived at the vicarage in Usk and in November 1892 she presented Miss Baker, daughter of the late Reverend S.C. Baker with an album full of views which had been subscribed for by a large number of parishioners. They were collected by Mrs Byrde, about a hundred views by the permanent platinum process and included interesting scenes in and around Usk and the county. Miss Baker was leaving for London.

Garden Party

A sale of work was held at Christchurch Vicarage in July 1903 in aid of the curacy fund. There was a good attendance and many parishioners and friends from all over Monmouthshire attended. All kinds of articles were sold on stalls set up under large trees and the Monmouthshire Central Advertiser stated that the ladies made 'excellent saleswomen'. The stallholders were – Miss Dorothy Mackworth and Miss Laybourne – Fancy work, Miss Taplin – plain work, Miss Florence Prothero and Mrs Coulman – China, Miss Lyne – pottery, the Misses Robinson – baskets, Mrs Miller – sweets, Miss

Agnes Evans – Art, Miss Cox and Miss Greenway – dairy.

DEATH

Sadly there are times during the research of women's history that the only time a woman is mentioned is when she dies, and only then because she was rich, had achieved a great age or had been involved in an accident.

Elizabeth Rees

On 3rd March 1841, at Waunwern Lodge, Pontypool, Elizabeth died, aged 102. She had nine children, forty grand children and fifty six great grand children. Newspaper, The Welshman recorded that her faculties remained unimpaired until the last. She had memories of Mr John Wesley, of him preaching at Carmarthen seventy years previously. She became a member of the Wesleyan movement and her last words were – 'In a short time I shall see Christ in all his fullness'. She died peacefully.

Mrs Hanbury Leigh

The funeral of Mrs Hanbury Leigh, lady of the Lord Lieutenant of Monmouthshire, held in high esteem for her many acts of kindness and charity took place on 7th July 1846 from Pontypool Park to Trevethin Church and the family vault. Around five hundred inhabitants of the town and neighbourhood dressed in mourning clothes and assembled in the park before joining the funeral procession which was headed by upward of one hundred tenants.

Inhabitants of the town also closed their houses as a mark of respect and it is estimated about ten thousand people lined the road from the park to the church.

Mrs Davies

In October 1856, George Lucas and two of his brothers were sailing up a river in their boat. They looked towards the riverbank and saw a shawl spread out on some sticks. On landing they found other items, a bonnet in a tree and a purse containing eighteen shillings and sixpence. On making inquiries it was found the items belonged to Mrs Davies who left her home in Penycaemawr, Newbridge and had disappeared. It was supposed she had drowned herself on account of her husband running up debts in Usk.

Mrs Carter

Mrs Carter, of Bolton Terrace, Newport died in June 1863. According to her family she had reached the age of a hundred and two though the breast plate on her coffin read a hundred and one. Nothing definite was known as to the date of her birth, everyone accepted the statement of Mrs Carter as to her age in years previous and this had been accepted as authentic. She was born in the hamlet of 'Masherne', near Chepstow though the parish records recorded nothing reliable about her birth. Even so it was agreed that however old she was, it was a great age.

Silvia Tiley

Silvia's funeral took place in April 1866. Her coffin was followed to the Penmaen cemetery by a large number of family and friends. Silvia was eighty seven years old and had been a consistent member of the Wesleyan Society for forty four years. She had four children, twenty five grand children and thirty nine great grand children

A Woman

A woman was found dead on the mountain between Abersychan and Abertillery in March 1867. She had been carrying a basket of shopping and it was thought she lost her way. She fell into a hollow and it was only because some men passing by heard her dog barking, that her body was discovered.

Mrs Hopkins

In October 1866, Mrs Hopkins, the wife of a barber, living in Dolphin Street, Newport was seized with Choleric diarrhoea. She died the same night and was buried first thing in the morning. It was an isolated incident, the only case occurring in the town in the previous three weeks.

Anne Williams

In Newport in April 1870, Mr W H Brewer held an inquest on the body of Anne who was described as a woman of loose character. From the examination he ascertained that Anne had recently given birth to an illegitimate child and that no midwife or doctor was present. It was supposed she became greatly exhausted and by the time the doctor had been sent for and arrived, she was past recovery. The jury returned a verdict to that effect.

Mary King

Mary was found in a dying state in October 1870 at a place known as the Snail Creep, between the Varteg and Cwmavon. Her skull and several ribs had been fractured. A verdict of 'Found dead' was returned with the suspicion of foul play

Mary Wilkins

An inquest was held as to the death of Mary in June 1872. She lived in Penygarn near Pontypool. The old lady was sitting by the fireside and reached forward to pick up her cup of tea which had been placed near to her. She then lost balance, fell forward against the bars of the grate which caused her neckerchief to catch fire. The flames quickly spread to her other clothes and despite the efforts of her grand daughter, Mary was so badly burned that she died twelve hours later.

Catherine Driscoll

Catherine, of James Court, Newport, fell downstairs and broke her neck in October 1872. She died before either medical or religious help could arrive. It appeared she had been to a Catholic christening and was drunk.

Charlotte Partridge

Charlotte of Cwmffrwd House, near Pontypool, was the widow of William Partridge. She died on the 18th March 1873 aged 62. She was held in high esteem by a large circle of friends and also well known and respected by the poor. She was always ready to help those less well off and it was said that no one left her door empty handed, she was a friend to all.

Mrs Hughes

In Ebbw Vale in October 1875, Mrs Hughes was crossing the railway line near the London and North Western Railway Station when a passing engine knocked her down and cut her head off. Her body lay on one side of the track and her head some distance away. An inquest was held at the Bridge End by Mr W H Brewer, the only witness was John Young whose evidence showed the accident was not caused by neglect on the part of the engine driver. A verdict of accidental death was returned.

Elizabeth Frances Webb

The Illustrated London News gave notice in December 1877 of the death of Miss Webb. She was lady of the manor of Wentsland and Bryngwyn which included Pontypool and Trevethin. She also owned estates in Monmouth. She died at 29 Chesham Place, London on 6th October and left an estate worth £70,000. She left the Abersychan Works and other mineral properties under lease to the Ebbw Vale Coal and Iron company to her cousin Sir William Vernon Guise Bart and his sister. Other estates were distributed to various relatives and she also left some of her property to servants, friends and charities.

Mrs Johns

On a Sunday evening in April 1878, Mrs Johns of Abertillery was in the act of opening the vestry door of Trinity Calvinistic Methodist chapel, where she was going to worship. She said, addressing a Mrs Henry James who accompanied her 'Oh dear, I have a pain in my head'. She then fell over and before she could be conveyed to her home, she died.

Margaret Davies

An inquest was held at the Crown Inn, Varteg by Mr E. D. Batt on the body of Margaret who had died very suddenly in February 1879. She was born on 6th November 1773 and so was in her hundred and sixth year. She lived on a farm in Cwmavon with her son Morgan Davies who said he saw her go to bed as usual at 8 p.m. Within about half an hour she had died. A verdict of death by natural causes and decay was returned.

Mrs Evans

In April 1880, Mrs Evans of Blackwood, wife of Richard Evans, a labourer, drowned herself. She went out of the house at five in the morning, leaving a note for her husband telling him and her dear children, goodbye. The note stated she would be found in the foundry pond.

Elizabeth Morgan

In January 1891, Elizabeth, died at the age of a hundred and five years. She had lived in Cwmbran for many years with her husband who survived her and who also was born in the same year. They both retained all their faculties in old age and Mr Morgan had nursed his wife through her ill health, though it had taken a toll on his own.

Mrs Woods

At ten o clock one December night in 1892, Mrs Woods, a young woman and wife of a collier died suddenly at her home in Chapel-of-Ease, Abercarn. She had eaten a 'hearty supper' and made no complaint but half an hour later she died before medical assistance could be obtained.

Mrs Williams

Recorded in the South Wales Daily News in December 1892 as Mrs Charles Williams, she travelled to South Africa a year previously to join her husband. Mrs Williams belonged to a highly respected family in the district and when she left was in full health and looking forward to the time when she would return to Abercarn and settle down. She was only ill for a few days and her death came as a great shock to the family.

Mrs Harris

Mrs Harris was a mother of seven children. In May 1893, while hanging out clothes at the back of her house in the Ranks, Abercarn, she fell down a short flight of steps and died within half an hour. Dr. Davies who quickly attended could find no marks of injury and so thought her death was caused by a stroke.

Muriel Griffiths

In January 1902, Mr M Roberts Jones, coroner conducted an inquiry at Abercarn police station concerning Muriel's death.

Miss Emily Banks, a nurse who attended Muriel during her confinement stated that Muriel had suffered from depression. On 10th January, she had given birth to a baby boy and was attended by D. Richards of Risca. Muriel then became very depressed and ate very little food.

On the night of her death, Muriel had had a long conversation with her husband, also a doctor. She then asked him to go downstairs away from her for a little while. Later, Dr. Griffiths left the house and the nurse, on going in to Muriel's room found her lying on the floor. She was retching violently. The nurse helped her back into bed when she threw up some coloured matter the nurse recognised as perchloride of mercury, two tablets of which had been left in the room for cleaning and sanitary purposes. They were in a small box in a room where other disinfectants were kept. Muriel told her husband on his return, she had only taken one. Everything was done to try and save Muriel but she died that night.

Dr. Richards stated he had known Muriel since she was a child and that she was twenty three. He said she did well after her confinement as far as he could see. She had been depressed before her marriage. He had been told that Dr. Griffiths was trying to cheer Muriel up as she had not been eating or sleeping well. When the nurse called him, he found Muriel lying across the bed in severe pain and vomiting. He then administered emetics and soon after, Dr. Griffiths returned. When Muriel regained consciousness she was asked if she had taken mercurial tablets, to which she replied 'yes'. These tablets contained corrosives and were used for antiseptic purposes and in small quantities for internal medicinal use. Dr Richards was sure Muriel suffered from puerperal melancholia and was unaccountable for her actions. The coroner and jury agreed and returned a verdict to that effect.

Winifred Matthews

Winifred, aged sixty one, of Abersychan, died in January 1909 as a result of burns. She had retired to bed on a Saturday night but when her husband and son returned home around 11 p.m. they found her lying unconscious on a mat beside the bed suffering from burns. Her clothes were still smouldering. A doctor was immediately called but she died the next morning. It was thought she had a fit and fell out of bed knocking over a candle which was placed on a small table which in turn ignited her clothes.

Elizabeth Jane Howe

At Abercarn police station in August 1910, Mr M. Roberts Jones, coroner investigated the death of Elizabeth, aged fifty three, caretaker of the Workmen's Club, Abercarn. Evidence showed that at two thirty in the morning, she was heard coughing violently. Dr. Dunlop was sent for but Mrs Howe died before he arrived. The daughter of Mrs Howe had had her clothes catch on fire the previous day and this had given her a severe shock. Dr. Dunlop said this might have caused her death. It was his opinion death was from natural causes and heart failure.

Elizabeth Harcourt Mitchell

Elizabeth was the wife of Colonel F.J. Mitchell of Llanfrechfa Grange. She died in September 1910 at the age of seventy six. She was very popular with local residents and as her funeral cortege passed, school children lined the road. She was described in the Cardiff Times as a 'true daughter of the county', she was interested in all that concerned its welfare and she was also a kind and generous friend who loved Monmouthshire's history and folklore. She belonged to the Monmouthshire and Caerleon Antiquarian Society and with her husband and their friend Octavius Morgan devoted a lot of time researching the county's history.

Elizabeth was an avid writer an created a list of her work though by her own admission 'There are other things which I have forgotten. If I remember them they can be added again'.

REFERENCES

Pontypool Free Press
Monmouthshire Merlin
Weekly Mail
Cardiff Times
Illustrated Usk Observer
Carmarthen Journal
South Wales Daily News
Evening Express
Pontypool Messenger
The Welshman
South Wales Echo

ABOUT THE AUTHOR

Carol Ann Lewis was born in Cwmbran in 1969. She attended Llantarnam
School where she had poetry lessons with Gillian Clarke. She wrote local
history articles for a Cwmbran newsletter and then became secretary of
Cwmbran Writers Group in 1999. She has had poems published in various
anthologies as well as in publications by Cwmbran Writers Group. She has
also studied Welsh history and heritage with the University of South Wales.

Printed in Great Britain
by Amazon